Fred. W. Kittermaster

Shropshire: Arms and Lineages

Salzwasser

Fred. W. Kittermaster

Shropshire: Arms and Lineages

1. Auflage | ISBN: 978-3-84605-600-4

Erscheinungsort: Frankfurt, Deutschland

Erscheinungsjahr: 2020

Salzwasser Verlag GmbH

Reprint of the original, first published in 1869.

SHROPSHIRE

ARMS AND LINEAGES:

COMPILED FROM

The Heralds' Visitations

AND

ANCIENT MSS.,

BY THE

REV. FRED. W. KITTERMASTER, M.A.,

Hon. Chaplain of the Shropshire Artillery Volunteers,
and sometime Vicar of Edgton.

———

LONDON:

WILLIAM MACINTOSH, PATERNOSTER ROW.

SHREWSBURY:

J. O. SANDFORD, HIGH STREET.

———

MDCCCLXIX.

BIRMINGHAM :

PRINTED BY WILLIAM RICKMAN KING, SWAN PASSAGE.

TO

MRS. PERRY,

OF

BRYN TANAT, MONTGOMERYSHIRE,

DESCENDED

PATERNALLY FROM THE EYTONS, OF EYTON,

AND

MATERNALLY FROM THE PLOWDENS, OF PLOWDEN,

NAMES SECOND TO NONE

AMONG THE

GENTLE FAMILIES OF PROUD SALOPIA,

THIS BOOK IS

WITH MUCH RESPECT AND GRATITUDE

DEDICATED

BY THE COMPILER.

PREFACE.

THE following collection of ARMS AND LINEAGES is an attempt
to ſhow what families belonged to the old gentry who were reſident
in the County of Salop before the year 1650. Theſe families for the
moſt part bore Arms, ſuch appendages being ever looked upon as an
evidence of gentle blood. In very early times perſons were allowed to
aſſume what Arms they pleaſed as military enſigns, and to grant them to
their retainers, and they were afterwards adopted as honorable diſtinctions.
When, however, they came to be regarded as an evidence of honor and
blood they were eagerly ſought after by all who roſe to places of truſt
or became poſſeſſors of property. The aſſumption of Arms at pleaſure
was, therefore, forbidden by royal authority, as early as the reign of
Hen. V., and no one was allowed to bear them unleſs they had them
by deſcent or grant. To this end the Kings of Arms were commiſſioned
by the Crown to make grants to fit perſons, under the authority of the
Earl Marſhal. And in order that none might bear them except thoſe
who had them by deſcent or grant, the Kings of Arms were authoriſed
to viſit their reſpective provinces, and to ſummon all who uſed them to
give ſatisfactory evidence of their right to do ſo. If the perſons ſum-
moned on theſe occaſions could eſtabliſh their claim, a record of the
family was entered in the Heralds' books. Theſe records are preſerved
in the Heralds' College, and in public and private libraries, and from

them moſt of the information in the following pages has been obtained. Perſons bearing Arms by deſcent from the old families ſhould be able to deduce an unbroken Lineage from ſome anceſtor whoſe claim has been allowed by the Heralds, and recorded in theſe documents.

The Viſitation commenced at a very early period—as early as the reign of Hen. IV. We find the following entry in one of the Harl MSS.: " Viſitacio faƈta per Mariſcballum de Norroy ult ann R. Henrici 4ti, 1412." The regular Viſitations, however, did not begin until early in the 16th century. Thomas Benolt, Clarenceux King of Arms, had a commiſſion granted 20 Hen. VIII., to viſit the Counties of Glouceſter, Worceſter, Oxford, Wilts, Bucks, and Stafford. After this the Viſitations were regularly made until the end of the 17th century, the laſt being that of Southampton, made by the Deputies of Sir Henry St. George Clarenceux, in the year 1686.

Viſitations of Shropſhire were made—

In 1567 by William Flower, Norroy.

In 1569 and 1584 by Robert Cooke, Clarenceux, and his Deputy, Richard Lee, Portcullis.

In 1623 by Robert Treſwell, Somerſet Herald, and Auguſtine Vincent, Rouge Croix, Deputies for William Camden, Clarenceux.

In 1663 by William Dugdale, Norroy, and Gregory King, Deputies for Sir Edward Byſſhe, Clarenceux.

The old form of ſpelling has been retained, and a diſtinguiſhing mark affixed to families which, according to Mr. Shirley, are of Knightly and Gentle deſcent.

In order to make the book one of reference, a circular was iſſued, not only to the repreſentatives of old families, but very generally to the gentry and profeffional men in Shrewfbury and in the County. Thofe who kindly gave the information required are inferted in the appendix. This information has not been compared with any heraldic record, but accepted folely on the authority of the perfons furnifhing it. It may be remarked, however, that in modern defcents tracing from ancient fources there is often much that is conjectural, but nothing ought to be received as of undoubted authority unlefs fupported by documentary evidence.

The compiler acknowledges his obligation to Dr. Kennedy and to Mr. Mofs for their permiffion to infpect the Vifitation in the School Library; alfo to Dr. Johnfon for the free accefs afforded to the valuable copy of fuch Vifitation and other MSS. (now in the Shrewfbury Mufeum) of the late George Morris.

ALL SAINTS, COVENTRY,
    SEPTEMBER, 1869.

ABBREVIATIONS, &c.

or.	gold or yellow.
arg.	filver or white.
az.	azure or blue.
gu.	gules or red.
vert	green.
purp.	purple.
fa.	fable or black.
erm.	ermine.
ppr.	proper.
betw.	between.
chev.	chevron.
engr.	engrailed.
guard.	guardant.
pafs.	paffant.
ramp.	rampant.
b.	born.
m.	married.
fuc.	fucceeded.
daug.	daughter.
d. and h.	daughter and heirefs.
d. and co-h.	daughter and co-heirefs.
Pr. Rep.	Prefent Reprefentative.
Her. Vis.	*Herald's Vifitation.*
Harl MS.	*Harleian Manufcript.*
Add. MS.	*Additional Manufcript.*
Qu. Coll. MS.	*Queen's College Manufcript.*
Morris MS.	*Manufcript of the late George Morris.*

*Affixed to Families of Knightly defcent.

†Affixed to Families of Gentle defcent.

SHROPSHIRE ARMS AND LINEAGES.

Acheley, or **Atcherley.**—Gu. on a fefs eng. arg., betw. three griffins' heads erased or., as many croffes formée fitchée fa.

Confirmed to Sir Roger Acheley, Lord Mayor of London, fon of Thomas Acheley, of Stanwardine. *Her. Vis.*

This Sir Roger is mentioned in " Fuller's Worthies," and in " Stow's Survey of London," as having munificently stored Leadenhall for the relief of the poor. He died 13 Hen. VIII.

Defcendants : The Miffes Atcherley, of Shrewfbury.

Through the female line—David Francis Atcherley, Efq., of Marton.

†**Acton.**—Gu. two lions pafs. arg., armed and langued gu., betw. nine croffes crofflet fitchée or. Creft : On a wreath a circular wreath arg. and gu., therein a leg in armour ppr., garnished or., bent at the knee and couped at the middle of the thigh, blood iffuing therefrom of the second.

•ↄ Confirmed (with 7 quarterings) to Walter Acton, of Aldenham (Sheriff 1630), 4th in defcent from John Acton, of the fame place, who was fon of Thomas Acton, of Longnor, 36 Hen. VI., and 3rd in defcent from Walter Acton, of the same place, a fon of Edward Acton, of Aldenham (Sheriff 1383), and grandfon of William, of Acton Burnell. *Her. Vis.* 1623. *Blakeway.*

Pr. Rep.: Sir John Emerich Edward Dalberg Acton, of Aldenham Park. 8th Baronet. Creation 1644.

Acton.—Quarterly, per fefs indented arg. and gu., in the first quarter a Cornish chough fa.

Confirmed (with 9 quarterings) to Edward Acton, of Acton Scott, 8th in defcent from Walter Acton, of the fame place, who was grand-fon of John le Scott, of Acton, 7 Edw. III., and 5th from Walter le Scott, 39 Hen. III., a fon of Thomas le Scott.

Her. Vis. 1623.   *Harl MS.*

Pr. Rep.: Through the female line—Auguftus Wood (great grandfon of Sufan, only child of Edward Acton, and wife of John Stackhoufe, of Pendarves), who will take the name of Acton on fucceeding to the eftate.

Acton.—Gu., a fefs within a border, both engr. erm.

Arms of Sir Roger Acton, Governor of Ludlow Caftle temp. Hen. IV., and Sheriff 1410.   *Blakeway.*

Adams.—Erm., a chev. vair or. and az., betw. three roses gu., seeded of the second. Crest: A griffin's head erased erm., beaked gu., charged with a chev. vair or. and az.

Confirmed to William Adams, of Cleeton, 3rd in defcent from William Adams, of the fame place.   *Her. Vis.*

Adams.—Erm., three cats a mountain pafs. guard. in pale az., tails coward. Creft: A greyhound's head erafed erm.

Confirmed (with 2 quarterings) to Francis Adams, of Longdon, 6th in defcent from William Adams, of the fame place, a fon of Richard Adams, of Kent.   *Her. Vis.* 1623.

Albaney.—Arg., on a fefs betw. three cinquefoils gu., a greyhound courant or. Creſt: Out of a ducal coronet gu., a demi-dolphin hauriant or.

Confirmed (with 3 quarterings) to Francis Albaney, of Whittington, brother of Sir Robert Albaney, of Bagſhott, Surrey, who was grandſon of William Albany.

Sheriff: Francis, 1595.   *Her. Vis.* 1623. *Blakeway.*

Alkington.—Quarterly, or. and gu., an eagle displayed counter-changed.

Confirmed to Roger Alkington, of Ofweſtry, grandſon of William Alkington, of Alkington.   *Her. Vis.*

Asturel or Asturelley.—Erm., on a bend gu., three efcallop shells arg.

Confirmed as the arms of Afturel or Afturelley.   *Harl MS.*

Atcherley, see **Acheley.**

Atkins.—Arg., a crofs cotifed flory betw. four mullets, all ſa.

Confirmed as the arms of Richard Atkins.   *Harl MS.*

Atwood.—Gu., a lion ramp., double queued or.

Confirmed to Samuel Atwood, of Broughton, 4th in defcent from John Atwood, of Atwood Park.   *Her. Vis.*

Bagshaw.—Or., a bugle horn ſa., betw. three rofes gu.

Confirmed to Thomas Bagſhaw, fon of Arthur Bagſhaw, who m. Ann, daug. of Henry Hinton.   *Harl MS.*

Baker.—Az., on a chev. or., betw. three fwans' heads erafed of the fecond, beaked gu., as many cinquefoils of the third.

Arms of Thomas Baker, of Swinney, Sheriff 1649, grandfon of Thomas Baker, of Bafchurch, defcended from the Bakers, of Kent.

Blakeway.

Baker.—Sa., a griffin fegreant erm., ducally gorged or., beaked and membered gu.

Arms of Baker.

John, fon of Thomas Baker, of Hanwood, was 5th in defcent from Thomas Baker. *Harl MS. Her. Vis.* 1623.

†**Baldwyn.**—Arg., a faltire fa. Creft: A cockatrice arg., wattled, combed, and beaked or., ducally gorged and lined of the laft.

Confirmed to Edward, grandfon of Nicholas Baldwyn, of Didlebury 1584, who was grandfon of John Baldwyn, of the fame place, temp. Edw. III., and 10th in defcent from John Baldwyn, of Didlebury. *Harl MS.*

Pr. Rep. :—William Lacon Childe, Efq., of Kinlet Hall, whofe father, William Baldwyn, affumed the name of Childe.

Banaster or **Banester.**—Arg., a crofs flory fa. Creft: A peacock ppr.

Confirmed to Rowland Banafter, of Lacon, 6th in defcent from Rauffe Banefter, of Laken.

Sheriff: Thomas, 1403. *Her. Vis. Blakeway.*

Barker.—Gu., a fefs compony or. and az., betw. six annulets of the fecond. Creft: A falcon arg., legged gu., beaked and billed or., wings expanded of the laft.

Granted by William Harvey, Clar., to James Barker, of Haghmond.

Confirmed (with 1 quartering) to his grandfon Walter Barker, of Haghmond, 1623.

Sheriffs: Rowland, 1585; Walter, 1621. *Her. Vis. Blakeway.*

Barker, or Coberall.—Az., five eſcallop ſhells in croſs or. Creſt : On a rock arg., a hawk cloſe or.

Confirmed (with 2 quarterings) to John Barker, of Hopton Caſtle, 4th in deſcent from John Barker, alias Coverall, of Coulhurſt, who was alſo grandfather of James Barker, of Haghmond. *Her. Vis.*

Barkley, or Berkley.—Gu., a chev. betw. ten croſſes pattée, ſix in chief and four in baſe, arg. Creſt : A mitre gu., charged with the arms.

Confirmed by Robert Cooke, Clar., to Thomas Berkley, of Ewdnes, 7th in deſcent from John Berkley, a younger ſon of Maurice Lord Berkley, temp. Edw. II.

Alſo to Francis Barkley, deſcended from Morris Lord Barkley.
Her. Vis. Harl MS.

Barnefield.—Or., on a bend gu., three mullets arg. Creſt : A lion's head eraſed ſa., ducally crowned gu.

Confirmed to William Barnefield, of Newport, grandſon of William Barnefield, of the ſame place, who was grandſon of Walter Barnefield, of Poulmore, Co. Devon. *Her. Vis.*

Barton.—Arg., a bend double cotiſed ſa.

Confirmed to Owen Barton, of Didleſton, ſon of Edward Lloyd Barton, of Bridleſton, who was great grandſon of Roger Barton. *Her. Vis.*

Barton.—Arms same as preceding.

Confirmed, 1592, as the arms of George Barton, ſon of Howell Barton, who m. Joane, d. and h. of Thomas Ball, of Malpas.
Harl MS.

Baskerbille.—Arg., a chev. gu., betw. three torteaux.

Confirmed as the arms of Humphrey Baskerville, Alderman of London, whoſe d. Sara m. Thomas Owen, of Shrewſbury.
Her. Vis.

Baugh.—Gu., a fefs vair betw. three mullets arg.
Creft: Out of a ducal coronet or., a talbot fejant fa.

Confirmed, 1588, to Thomas Baugh, of Aldencourt, fon of John
Baugh, of the fame place. *Her. Vis.*

Bayllie.—Vert, a chev. or., betw. three unicorns' heads
erafed arg., armed of the fecond.

Confirmed, 1584, (with 1 quartering) to John Bayllie, of Shrewfbury,
grandfon of John Bayllie. *Harl MS.*

Beeston.—Arg., a bend betw. fix bees fa.

Confirmed to Randall Beefton, of Salop, fon of Richard Beefton, of
the fame place, and grandfon of Randall Beefton, of Beefton, Chefhire.
Harl MS.

Beift.—Gu., three bundles of arrows arg. Creft: An
arm embowed holding a bow.

Confirmed to William Beift, of Acham, fon of Roger Beift, of the
fame place. *Her. Vis.*

Bembow.—Sa., two ftringed bows endorfed in pale or.,
garnifhed gu., betw. two bundles of arrows, five and
four, in fefs or., barbed and headed arg., tied up gu.
Creft: A harpy clofe or., face ppr., her head wreathed
with a chaplet of flowers gu.

Granted by William Camden, Clar.
Confirmed to John Bembow, of Newport and of London, 4th in
defcent from Roger Bembow, of Newport. *Her. Vis.*

Benion or **Ap Einion.**—Erm., a chev. fa., in chief or.,
a lion pafs gu.

Confirmed as the arms of Richard ap Einion, of Salop.
Harl MS.

Bennett.—Per bend dancetteé arg. and fa., a bend betw. two martlets counter-changed.

Confirmed as the arms of Bennett. *Harl MS.*

Bentall or Benthall.—Or., a lion ramp., double queued az., ducally crowned gu. Creft: On a ducal coronet or., a leopard ftatant arg., fpotted fa.

Confirmed (with 2 quarterings) to Lawrence, fon of John Bentall, of Bentall, 9th in defcent from Walter de Bentall, Juxta Wenlock, who was the fon of Philip Bentall, and 7th from Roger Bentall, of Bentall.

This family was fettled at Benthall Edge foon after the Conqueft. In 1280, Margery, d. and co-h. of Philip de Benthall, m. John Burnell, of Acton Burnell, who afterwards took the name of Benthall or Bentall.

Her. Vis. Harl MS.

Pr. Rep.: William Benthall, Efq., of Totnefs, and Buckfaft Abbey.

Defcendants: His brothers—John, Vicar of Willen—Edward, of Sherborne—Henry—Francis—Octavius.

Alfo, Edward Hammond Bentall, Efq., M.P. for Maldon.

Berington.—Az., three greyhounds courant in pale fa., collared gu., within a border of the laft.

Confirmed to Thomas Berington, of Mothall, fon of Roger Berington, of Shrewfbury, 7th' in defcent from Roger Berington, who m. Alice, daug. of John Ireland, fon of Sir Walter Fitzroy, of Ireland, who was fon of Edw. I. by a daug. of the Earl of Kildare. *Her. Vis. 1623.*

Berry.—Erm., on a bend az., three fleurs-de-lis or..

Confirmed to Thomas Berry, of Ludlow, grandfon of John Berry, Co. Devon. *Her. Vis. 1623.*

†𝕭𝖊𝖙𝖙𝖔𝖓.—Arg., two pales ſa., each charged with three
croſſes croſſlet fitchée or.

Confirmed to Richard Betton, of Berwick, 4th in deſcent from
Thomas Betton, of Berwick.

Richard Betton was deſcended from William Betton, of Berwick,
temp. Hen. IV., 4th in deſcent from Walter le Betton, of Betton Strange,
temp. Edw. I.   *Her. Vis. Shirley.*

Pr. Rep. : Richard Betton, Eſq., Overton Houſe, Ludlow.

𝕭𝖎𝖑𝖑𝖎𝖓𝖌𝖘𝖑𝖊𝖞.—Arg., a croſs ſa., voided of the field, five lions
ramp. reversed in croſs of the ſecond, (armed and
langued gu.,) betw. four lions ramp. of the ſecond.
Creſt: On a mount vert, a leopard couchant arg.,
ſpotted ſa.

Confirmed to Francis Billingſley, 4th in deſcent from William
Billingſley.   *Her. Vis.* 1623.

𝕭𝖎𝖑𝖑𝖎𝖓𝖌𝖘𝖑𝖊𝖞.—Gu., a fleur-de-lis or., a canton of the ſecond.
Creſt: On a mount vert, a leopard couchant ſpotted ſa.

Confirmed (with 1 quartering) to Sir Henry Billingſley, Lord Mayor
of London, 5th in deſcent from Roger Billingſley, of Billingſley.

                                 Her. Vis.

𝕭𝖎𝖗𝖈𝖍.—Arg., a chev. betw. three mullets ſa. Creſt: A
demi-bird with wings diſplayed ſa.

Confirmed to Abel Birch, of Ludlow, 4th in deſcent from Henry
Birch, of Birch Hall, Co. Lancaſter.   *Her. Vis.*

𝕭𝖑𝖆𝖓𝖈𝖒𝖎𝖓𝖘𝖙𝖊𝖗.—Arg., a fret gu.

Confirmed as the arms of Blancminſter, of Salop.   *Harl MS.*

Blonden or **Blunden**.—Arg., a lion paſs. guard. az. Creſt: A demi-griffin or., gorged with a feſs erm.

Confirmed (with 2 quarterings) by Sir William Camden, Clar., to Richard Blunden, of Biſhop's Caſtle, 11th in deſcent from Sir Robert Blunden, temp. Hen. III. *Harl MS.*

Blount or **Blunt**.—Nebulée of ſix or. and ſa. Creſt: On a chapeau gu., turned up erm., a lion paſs. az., ducally crowned or.

Confirmed (with 28 quarterings) as the arms of Walter Blount, of Sodington, 7th in deſcent from Sir Walter Blount, of the ſame place, temp. Edw. I., grandſon of Sir William Blount.

Alſo, as the arms of Sir George Blount, of Kinlet, 4th in deſcent from John Blount, of the ſame place, who was 3rd from Walter Blount, of Sodington, temp. Edw. I.

Sheriffs: Humphrey, 1461; Thomas, 1480; Edward, 1489; Thomas, 1519; George, 1564. *Her. Vis. Blakeway.*

Blount or **Blunt**.—Same arms as preceding. Creſt: A gauntlet in the ſun ppr.

Confirmed (with 2 quarterings) as the arms of Walter Blount, of Stretton, who m. Mary, daug. of Lord Brabazon, of Ireland, 1623, and 4th in deſcent from John Blount, of Yeo, who was ſon of Sir Humphrey Blount, of Kinlet. *Her. Vis.*

Blyke.—Sa., a chev. betw. three leopards' heads arg.

Confirmed as the arms of Blyke, of Aſtley. *Harl MS.*

Bohun.—Az., on a bend arg., cotiſed or., ſix lions ramp. of the third.

Confirmed to Sir John Bohun, 4th ſon of Humphrey, 8th Earl of Hereford. *Harl MS.*

Boothe.—Arg., a rose gu., betw. three boars' heads erect and erased sa.

Confirmed to Thomas Boothe, of Shiffnal, grandson of Oliver Boothe, Co. Derby.   *Harl MS.*

Bostock.—Sa., on a humet arg., a martlet arg. (or.) Crest: A martlet as in the shield.

Confirmed (with 1 quartering) to Hugh Bostock, of Moreton Say, who m. Margaret, daug. of Thomas Lee, of Langley.   *Harl MS.*

Boteler.—Gu., a fess chequy or. and sa., betw. six crosses crosslet arg. Crest: An arm embowed in armour or. and arg., holding a sword of the last, hilt sa.

Confirmed to Thomas Boteler, of Ludlow, who m. Eliza, daug. of Thomas Burnaby, of Hill, Co. Worcester.   *Harl MS.*

Boterell.—Arg., a lion ramp. sa., a chief gu.

Confirmed to Thomas Boterell, of Boterell's Aston, 9th in descent from John Boterell, temp. Edw. II., who was grandson of Sir Thomas Boterell, of the same place.   *Harl MS.*

Botbille, see **Thinne.**

Bowdler.—Arg., two birds in pale sa., beaked and legged gu.

Confirmed to William, son of Richard Bowdler, of Ludlow.

Also to Sir Stephen Bowdler, of Hope Bowdler, 4th in descent from John Bowdler, of the same place.   *Her. Vis.*

Also to Samuel Bowdler, of Salop and Arlescot, son of Roger Bowdler, of Oswestry, 4th son of John Bowdler, of Salop, who was great-grandson of Hugh Bowdler, of Hope Bowdler.   *Her. Vis.*

Bridgeman.—Az., ten bezants on a chief arg., a lion paſs ſa.

Confirmed to William Bridgeman, 4th in deſcent from Thomas Bridgeman, Co. Suffolk. *Her. Vis.*

Briggs.—Gu., three bars gemelles or., a canton ſa., charged with a creſcent or. Creſt: On the ſtump of a tree a pelican or., wings endorſed, vulning herſelf ppr.

Confirmed (with 2 quarterings) to Oliver Briggs, of Erneſtree, grand-ſon of Symon Briggs, who was 5th in deſcent from John Briggs, Lord of De Hall, Co. Norfolk. *Harl MS. Her. Vis.* 1623.

Brockwell.—Sa., three nags' heads eraſed arg.

Confirmed (with 5 quarterings) as the arms of Brockwell. *Harl MS.*

Brome.—Az., a hand erect in pale, couped at the wriſt arg. Creſt: An armed arm, veſted gu., turned up arg., holding in the hand ppr., a ſlip of broom vert, flowered or.

Confirmed to John Brome, 3rd in deſcent from William Brome, of Brome, gent. *Add. MS.*

Bromley.—Quarterly per feſs indented gu. and or., an eſcutcheon arg., charged with a griffin ſegreant vert. Creſt: Out of a ducal coronet or., a demi-lion arg., ſupporting a banner gu., charged with a lion paſs. gold, ſtaff of the laſt.

Confirmed (with 6 quarterings) by Robert Cooke, Clar., to Sir George Bromley, Juſtice of Cheſhire 1581, grandſon of William Bromley, of Metley, who was 10th in deſcent from Sir Walter Bromley, of Bromlegh, Sheriffs: William, 1229; John, 1405; George, 1522. *Her. Vis. Blakeway.*

Bromley.—Same arms as preceding. Creft: A pheafant fitting ppr.

Confirmed (with 2 quarterings) to Henry Bromley, of Shrawardine, 3rd in defcent from Sir Thomas Bromley, Chancellor of England 1581, who was brother of Sir George Bromley, Juftice of Chefhire 1581.

Her. Vis.

Broome.—Az., a hand erect betw.'three fleurs-de-lis arg.

Confirmed as the arms of Edward Broome, of Hopefay.

Alfo—Az., a hand erect arg. (betw. three broom flips ppr.)

Confirmed to Matthew Brome, of Hopefay, 1598, fon of Thomas Brome, of Afton, 3rd in defcent from William Brome, of Brome.

Harl MS.

Brooke.—Chequy arg. and fa. Creft: On a mount vert, a brock pafs. ppr.

Confirmed (with 3 quarterings) to Edward Brooke, of Church Stretton, grandfon of Francis Brooke, of Blakeland, Co. Stafford, 5th fon of John Brooke, of Boventon, Co. Stafford, who was 5th in defcent from Richard Brooke, of Cloreby. *Her. Vis. 1623.*

Brooke.—Chequy arg. and fa., on a chief or., a brock pafs. ppr. Creft: A heron or.

Granted by Robert Cooke, Clar., 1587. *Add. MS.*

Broughton.—Sa., a chev. betw. three owls arg.

Confirmed as the arms of Broughton. *Harl MS.*

Broughton.—Arg., two bars gu., on a canton of the firft, a faltire of the fecond. Creft: A talbot pafs. gu.

Confirmed (with 6 quarterings) to Richard Broughton, of Hanley, 3rd in defcent from Walter Broughton, of Broughton, who was 5th from Sir Walter Broughton, of the fame place. *Her. Vis.*

Browne.—Arg. a chev. betw. three mullets fa.

Confirmed to Thomas Browne, of Morfe, 4th in defcent from Alexander Browne, of the fame place. *Her. Vis.*

Bruyn.—Arg., an eagle difplayed fa., charged on the breaft with a fleur-de-lis or.

Arms of John Bruyn, of Bridgnorth; Sheriff 1420. *Blakeway.*

Bulkeley.—Sa., a chev. betw. three bulls' heads cabolfed arg. Creft : Out of a ducal coronet or., a bull's head arg., armed of the firft.

Arms of Robert Bulkeley, of Alle Stanefton, whofe daug. Ellena m. William Wettenhall. *Her. Vis.*

Burgh.—Az., three fleurs-de-lis erm.

Arms of Sir John Burgh, Sheriff 1442, fon of Hugh Burgh, Sheriff 1430, probably defcended from Hubert de Burgh, Earl of Kent. *Blakeway.*

Burley.—Arg., a lion ramp. fa., debruifed with a fefs chequy or. and az.

Confirmed as the arms of Burley.

Sheriffs : John, 1409; William, 1426.

Harl MS. Blakeway.

Burley.—Paly of fix fa. and or., on a chief of the fecond, two pallets of the firft, an efcutcheon, barry of fix gu. and erm.

Arms of Sir John Burley, whofe daug. Elizabeth m. Sir John Hopton. *Her. Vis.*

Burnell.—Arg., a lion ramp. fa., ducally crowned or., within a border az.

Confirmed as the arms of Hugh Burnell, Baron of Holgate, temp. Hen. V., whofe d. and h. Catherine m. Sir John Ratcliff. Hugh Burnell was 12th in defcent from Robert Burnell, who came to England with William the Conqueror, and was buried at Buildwas 1087.

Alfo to Richard Burnell, fon of Robert, who died 1593, and who was 13th from Hugh Burnell. *Her. Vis.*

Burton.—Per pale az. and purp., a crofs engr. or., betw. four rofes arg. (counterchanged.) Creft: A dexter gauntlet ppr., fhowing the infide of the hand.

Granted by John Wrythe, Norroy, May 22, 1478, to Robert Burton, Co. York.

Confirmed to Thomas Burton, fon of Edward Burton, of Longner, a grandfon of Edward Burton. This Edward Burton was the fon of Robert, temp. Hen. VII., and came out of Yorkfhire.

Sheriffs: John, 1353; Edmund, 1371.

Add. MS. Morris MS. Blakeway.

Pr. Rep.: Through the female line—Robert Lingen Burton, Efq., of Longner Hall.

Butler.—Gu., a fefs chequy arg. and fa., betw. fix croffes formée fitchée of the fecond.

Arms of Butler, Baron Wenne. *Harl MS.*

Chambers or **Chambre.**—Az., an armed arm, embowed or., iffuing from the finifter, holding a red rofe, flipped and leaved ppr. Creft: A greyhound's head erafed arg., round the neck a collar az., ring and buckle or.

Confirmed (with 2 quarterings) to Arthur Chambers, of Petton, grandfon of Richard Chambers, of the fame place, fon of Jenkin Chambers, of Burlton, who was 3rd fon of William Chambre, and 8th in defcent from John de Chambre. *Her. Vis.*

Pr. Rep.: Through the female line—Robert Chambre Vaughan, Efq., of Burlton.

Charlton.—Or., a lion ramp. gu.　Creft: A leopard's face erafed at the neck or.

Confirmed (with 2 quarterings) to Robert Charlton, of Tern, grandfon of Richard Charlton, 2nd fon of William Charlton, of Apley.

Alfo the arms of Edward Charlton, Lord of Powis, ob. 1420, whofe d. and co-h. Johanna m. Sir John Grey, Lord of Powys.

Sheriffs: Robert, 1472; Thomas, 1567; Andrew, 1590; Francis, 1626.　　　　　　　　　　*Her. Vis. Blakeway.*

Pr. Rep.: St. John Chiverton Charlton, Efq.

Chelmick or **Chelminke.**—Vert, three lions ramp. guard. or.　Creft: A lion fejant guard. or., holding in his dexter paw a fhield vert.

Confirmed to William Chelmick, of Chelmick, grandfon of William Chelmick, of Chelmick and Ragdon.　　　*Her. Vis. 1623.*

Clench.—Gu., a faltire or.

Arms (with 1 quartering) of William Clench, of Bridgnorth (fon of Nicholas Clench, of Dublin), who m. Frances, daug. of Richard Creffet, of Upton Creffet.　　　　　　　　　　*Add. MS.*

Chetilton.—Arg., on a chev. gu., five bezants all within a border engr. of the fecond.

Arms of William de Chetilton, whofe daug. Amabilla m. William Bromley, of Badington.　　　　　　　　*Harl MS.*

Church.—Arg., on a chev. gu., betw. three greyhounds' heads erafed fa., as many bezants.　Creft: A greyhound's head erafed, collared and ringed or.

Confirmed to William Church, of Betton, grandfon of William Church, of Nantwich, Co. Chefter.　　　*Her. Vis. 1623.*

Clarke.—Az., three efcallops in pale or., betw. two flaunches erm., on a chief arg., three lions ramp. guard. of the field.

Confirmed to Nicholas Clarke, of Shrewfbury, 3rd in defcent from Richard Clarke, of the fame place. *Her. Vis.* 1623.

Clay.—Per pale vert and fa., a lion ramp. erm., betw. three efcallops arg. Creft: A lion's head per pale vert and fa., charged with an efcallop arg.

Confirmed as the arms of George Clay, 3rd in defcent from Robert Clay, of Prees. *Her. Vis.* 1623.

Clibe, fee **Clybe.**

Clough.—Gu., three pine apples arg., leaved and ftalked ppr.

Confirmed to Francis Clough, of Minfterley, 7th in defcent from Hugh Clough, of the fame place. *Her. Vis.* 1623.

Cludd.—Erm., a fret fa. Creft: An eagle with wings expanded ppr., preying on a coney arg.

Confirmed (with 4 quarterings) to Edward, fon of Edward Cludd, of Orleton, 5th in defcent from William Cludd, 5 Hen. VI., and 9th from William Cludd, temp. Edw. III., a fon of Richard Cludd.
Harl MS.
Pr. Rep.: Through the female line—Anna Maria d. and h. of Edward Cludde, of Orleton, who m. the Hon. Robert Charles Herbert, 4th fon of Edward, 2nd Earl of Powis.

Clun.—Arg., a chief az. Creft: A chevalier in full armour, with a batôn in his hand ppr.

Thomas Clun was 4th in defcent from John Clun, of Clun.
Her. Vis.

†𝕮𝖑𝖞𝖇𝖊 or 𝕮𝖑𝖎𝖇𝖊.—Arg., on a fefs betw. three wolves' heads erafed fa., as many mullets or. Creft: A wolf's head erafed, per pale dancettée arg. and fa.

Confirmed (with 13 quarterings) to George Clyve, of Huxley, Co. Chefter, and of Stuche, grandfon of Richard Clyve, Lord of Huxley and Stuche, who was 8th in defcent from Stephen Clyve.

Her. Vis.

Pr. Rep.: Edward James Herbert, 3rd Earl of Powis.

𝕮𝖔𝖑𝖑𝖎𝖓𝖘.—Vert., a griffin fegreant or. Creft: A demi-griffin fegreant or., wings endorfed, collared erm.

Confirmed (with 1 quartering) to Richard Collins, grandfon of John Collins, of Dovehills, 2nd fon of Richard Collins, of Woodhide, Co. Hereford, 9th in defcent from Sir Peter Collins.

Her. Vis. 1623.

𝕮𝖔𝖓𝖎𝖓𝖌𝖘𝖇𝖞.—Gu., three conies fejant arg. Creft: A coney as in the arms.

Confirmed (with 9 quarterings) to Humphrey Coningfby, of Nene Solers, 7th in defcent from Sir William Coningfby, temp. Edw. III., fon of Roger Coningfby, of Moreton Bagott, Co. Warw.

Her. Vis. 1623.

𝕮𝖔𝖓𝖘𝖙𝖆𝖓𝖙𝖎𝖓𝖊.—Or., fix fleurs-de-lis fa., three, two, and one.

Granted by Cooke, Clar., 12th July, 1575.

Confirmed to Richard Conftantine, of Brodeley, grandfon of William Conftantine, of Whitchurch, who was 2nd fon of Thomas Conftantine, of Dodington. *Her. Vis.*

𝕮𝖔𝖔𝖕𝖊𝖗.—Arg, three plates on a bend betw. two lions ramp fa., all within a border engr. gu.

Confirmed to Richard Cooper, of Stanton, 1598, grandfon of Thomas Cooper, of Steventon. *Harl MS.*

*Corbett.—Or., a raven ſa.   Creſt: An elephant arg., armed gold, on his back a caſtle triple towered of the laſt, trappings or. and ſa.   Another—A ſquirrel ſejant or.

Confirmed (with 21 quarterings) to Sir Andrew Corbett, of Morton, grandſon of Sir Andrew (Sheriff 1551), ſon of Sir Roger (Sheriff 1550), who was grandſon of Sir Richard (Sheriff 1507), and 4th in deſcent from Robert (Sheriff 1419), and 8th from Sir Robert (Sheriff 1288), a grandſon of Sir Richard, of Watleſburgh and Moreton (temp. King John), who m. Joanna, d. and h. of Bartholomew Foret or Moreton, a deſcendant of Foret, Saxon Lord of Wroxeter (temp. Hen. I.)   This Sir Richard was 4th from Roger, ſon of Corbett the Norman.

Her. Vis. 1623.   *Harl MS.*   *Blakeway.*   *Eyton.*

Pr. Rep.: Sir Vincent Rowland Corbet, Bart., of Acton Reynald, 3rd Baronet.

*Corbett.—Or., two ravens in pale ppr.

The arms of Peter Corbett, Baron of Caus, temp. Edw. I., ſon of Thomas Corbett, Sheriff 1249, and 5th in deſcent from William Corbett, of Watleſburgh, who was ſon of Roger Corbett, and grandſon of Corbett the Norman.

Another deſcent makes this Peter great-grandſon of Symon, the ſon of Symon, and grandſon of Roger, the ſon of Corbett the Norman.

Her. Vis. 1623.   *Harl.*   *Eyton.*

*Corbett.—Or., two ravens in pale ppr., within a border engr. gu. (ſa.), bezantée of ten.   Creſt: A Corniſh chough ppr., holding in its beak a branch of holly vert, fructed gu.

Confirmed (with 3 quarterings) to Thomas Corbett, of Longnor, 11th in deſcent from William Corbett, of Acley, a ſon of Robert Corbett, of Caus Caſtle, and grandſon of William Corbett, of Watleſburgh.

Her. Vis.

Pr. Rep.: Through the female line—Lieut.-Col. Edward Corbett, M.P., of Longnor Hall.

*Corbett.—Or., two ravens in pale fa., within a border engr. gu.

Confirmed to William Corbett, of Leigh, 12th in defcent from Roger Corbett, of the fame place, who was fon of Robert Corbett, of Caus Caftle, the fon of William Corbett, of Watlefburgh.

Sheriff: Thomas, 1427. *Her. Vis.* 1623. *Blakeway.*

Defcendant: Through the female line—Rev. John Dryden Pigott-Corbet, of Sundorne Caftle.

*Corbet.—Or., three ravens in pale ppr.

The arms of Sir Robert Corbet, Sheriff 1454.

Alfo of Sir Robert Corbet, Sheriff 1414, great-grandfon of Thomas, Sheriff 1298. *Blakeway.*

*Cornwall.—Erm., a lion ramp. (reguard.) gu., crowned or., within a border engr. fa., bezantée.

The arms of Sir Brian Cornwall, of Kinlet (Sheriff 1378), whofe d. and h. Ifabel m. Sir John Blount, of Sodington. *Her. Vis.* 1623.

*Cornwall.—Arms as preceding.

Edmund Cornwall, Baron of Burford (Sheriff 1580), fon of Richard, Sheriff 1549, a defcendant of Sir Thomas Cornwall, Baron of Burford (Sheriff 1506), and grandfon of Thomas Cornwall, Baron of Burford (Sheriff 1459), who was 5th in defcent from Sir Geoffry de Cornwaill, younger brother of Edmund, the father of Brian de Cornwaill (Sheriff 1378). *Blakeway.*

Pr. Rep.: Herbert S. H. Cornewall, Efq., of Delbury.

Cofton.—Arg., a faltire vert, on a chief gu., a lion pafs. of the firft.

Confirmed to John Cofton, of Cofton, whofe daug. Alice m. 1ft Thomas Cludd, 2nd Richard Lawley. *Add. MS.*

Cotes.—Quarterly, firſt and fourth, paly of ſix or. and gu., ſecond and third erm. Creſt: A cock ppr., beaked, combed, and wattled or.

Confirmed (with 8 quarterings) to John Cotes, of Woodcote, (Sheriff 1614.) 3rd in deſcent from Humphrey Cotes, who was killed at Boſworth Field, and 6th from Sir Thomas Cotes, Lord of Cotes, temp. Hen. IV., and 15th from Richard de Cotes.

Her. Vis. 1623. *Blakeway.*

Pr. Rep.: John Cotes, Eſq., of Woodcote.

Cottingham.—Sa., two hinds counter-trippant in feſs arg.

Confirmed to William Cottingham of Trevaleen, 3rd in deſcent from George Cottingham, of Wrenbury, Co. Cheſter. *Her. Vis.*

Cotton.—Az., a chev. betw. three hanks of cotton arg.

Arms of Rowland Cotton, of Cotton, (Sheriff 1617), 9th in deſcent from Roger de Coton, of Coton. *Blakeway.*

Coverall, ſee **Barker.**

Cox.—Arg., a bend az., in the finiſter chief an oak leaf of the ſecond.

Confirmed to Robert Cox, of Bramfield, grandſon of Roger Cox, of Cantilupe. *Her. Vis.* 1623.

Cressett.—Az., a croſs engr. within a border alſo engr. or. Creſt: A demi-lion ramp. guard. arg., ducally crowned or., holding a beacon arg., fire ppr.

Confirmed (with 6 quarterings) to Edward Creſſett, of Upton, 4th in deſcent from Robert Creſſett, of Upton Creſſett.

Sheriffs: Hugh, 1435; Robert, 1469; Richard, 1584.

Her. Vis. 1623. *Blakeway.*

Crompton.—Gu., a fefs wavy betw. three lions ramp. or. Creft: A talbot fejant or., holding in his dexter paw a coil of rope arg.

Confirmed to Fulke 'Crompton, of Dawley Caftle, fon of Thomas Crompton, of Acton Burnell. *Her. Vis.*

Crowther.—Gu., a bend wavy vair.

Confirmed (with 7 quarterings) to Arthur Crowther, of London, who m. Mary, d. and h. of Geffrey Broughton. *Harl MS.*

Dannatt.—Sa., guttée arg., a canton of the fecond. Creft: A greyhound's head erafed arg., gorged with collar or., charged with three torteaux.

Confirmed to Sir John Dannatt, 6th in defcent from William Dannatt, of Weft Hope. *Her. Vis.*

Davenport.—Arg., a chev. betw. three croffes crofflet fitchée fa.

Confirmed to William Davenport, of Hawne, who m. Jane, s. and h. of Thomas Bromley, a grandfon of Sir George Bromley, of Chefter.
Harl MS.

Davies.—Sa., a goat arg., attired or., ftanding on a child ppr., fwaddled gu., and feeding on a tree vert.

Confirmed (with 1 quartering) to James Davies, 5th in defcent from Hugh Davies, fon of David, Co. Montgomery. *Her. Vis.*

Day.—Per chev. or. and az., three mullets counterchanged.

Confirmed to Richard Day, grandfon of Richard Day, of Worsfield.
Her. Vis.

Dodd.—Arg., on a fefs gu., betw. two cotifes wavy fa., three crefcents or. Creft: A ferpent az., iffuing from and piercing a garb or.

Confirmed to Richard Dodd, 4th in defcent from John Dodd, of Broxton, Co. Chefter.   *Her. Vis.*

†**Dodd.**—Arg., a fefs gu., betw. two cotifes wavy fa.

Confirmed (with 2 quarterings) to Richard Dodd, of Cloverley, 4th in defcent from William Dodd, of the fame place, who was grandfon of John Dodd, of Knoles.   *Her. Vis.*

Pr. Rep.: Whitehall Dod, Efq., Llannerch Park, Denbighfhire.

Dodington.—Az., a fefs betw. two mullets pierced in chief, and a chev. in bafe, or., within a border engr. az. Creft: A lion's gamb erect or.

Confirmed (with 3 quarterings) to George Dodington, of Dodington, 12th in defcent from John Dodington.   *Her. Vis.*

Downton.—Arg., three piles fa., on each a goat's head erafed of the firft, attired or. Creft: A dexter hand holding up a favage's head, transfixed with a fword in pale, all ppr.

Arms of Downton.   *Harl MS.*

Draper.—Bendy of eight gu. and vert, over all three fleurs-de-lis or.

Granted by William Camden, Clar.

Confirmed (with 1 quartering) to Humphrey Draper, of Bronflow and Afton, 4th in defcent from John Draper, of Afton.   *Her. Vis.*

Dychefield or **Dycher.**—Az., three pine apples or. Creſt: A bear paſs. arg.

Confirmed (with 3 quarterings) to Robert Dychefield, 4th in deſcent from Richard Dichfield, or Dycher, of Shawbarie and Mugleton.

Her. Vis. 1623.

Edge or **Hawkins.**—Arg., a hawk ppr. (beaked and legged or.), ſtanding on a ſtaff, couped and raguly vert.

Confirmed to Roger Edge or Hawkins, grandſon of William Edge or Hawkins. *Her. Vis.*

†**Edwardes.**—Gu., a chev. engr. betw. three heraldic tigers' heads eraſed at the neck arg. Creſt: A man's head armed in a helmet, ſide faced, all ppr.

Confirmed (with 1 quartering) to Thomas Edwardes, of Shrewſbury, ſon of Hugh Edwardes, of Kilhendre. This Thomas Edwardes was deſcended from Iddon, ſon of Rys Sais, a powerful Britiſh Chieftain in the Shropſhire Marches, and the family was ſeated at Kilhendre in the reign of Hen. I. *Her. Vis.* 1623. *Shirley.*

Pr. Rep.: Sir Henry Hope Edwardes, 10th Baronet, Wootton Hall, Aſhbourne.

Edwards.—Per bend ſiniſter erm. and ermines, over all a lion ramp or. Creſt: A man's head ſide-faced in a helmet, all ppr.

Confirmed (with 11 quarterings) as the arms of Vincent Edwards, of Lea, ſecond ſon of Thomas Edwards, of Liddame and Tickleton, who was 7th in deſcent from Ednouet, 4th ſon of Jerworth Voel.

Her. Vis. 1623.

Egerton.—(Arg.) a lion ramp. betw. three pheons (fa.) Creft: A lion ramp. (gu.) holding an arrow, point downwards fa., feathered arg.

Confirmed (with 1 quartering) to John Egerton, Vifcount Brackley, grandfon of Sir Thomas Egerton, Baron of Ellefmore, Vifcount Brackley, Lord Chancellor of England. *Her. Vis.*

Egerton, fee **Shepard.**

Einnes, fee **Heynes.**

Erdington.—Az. two lions pafs. or.

Arms of ——— Erdington, of Shawbury, whofe daug. Margaret m. Roger Corbet, of Morton. *Her. Vis.* 1623.

Evans.—Sa., a fefs. betw. three fleurs-de-lis or. Creft: An arm embowed and erect vefted az., cuffed or., holding in the hand a pink or gillyflower, all ppr.

Exemplified under the hand and feale of Sir William Dethick, Garter, to Thomas Evans, of Ofwaldeftree.

Confirmed to Edward Evans, of Trevelith, grandfon of the above Thomas Evans. *Her. Vis. Harl MS.*

Evans.—Or., a crofs moline betw. four lozenges az.

Confirmed (with 1 quartering) to Thomas Evans, of Shrewfbury, Captain of the Salop Volunteers, 4th in defcent from Hugh Evans, a defcendant of Jerworth, fon of the Lord of Melyenith, Ao. 978. *Harl MS.*

Eyton.—Erm., a lion ramp. az.

Confirmed (with 11 quarterings) to James Eyton, of Dudlefton, 5th in defcent from John Eyton, Ao. 1477, and 10th from Llewellyn ap Gruffith de Eiton, who was 4th from Elyder ap Rees Say. *Her. Vis.* 1623.

†**Eyton.**—Or., a fret az., quartered with gu., two bars erm. Creſt: A reindeer's head or., in his mouth an acorn ſlipped vert, fructed of the firſt. Another—A bird's head eraſed, holding in the beak a trefoil ſlipped, all ppr.

Confirmed (with 1 quartering) to Richard Eyton, of Eyton, Ao. 1608, 7th in deſcent from Sir George Eyton, ſon of Humphrey Eyton, who was a younger brother of John (Sheriff 1394), and ſon of Peter, and 7th from Peter de Eyton, 1194, ſon of Robert de Eyton, temp. Hen. II. This Robert was the probable deſcendant of Warin, Chief Feoffee in Shropſhire of William Pantulf, who held Eyton under the Norman Earl. The deſcendants of Robert bore the arms of Pantulf, Warin being probably a Cadet of the houſe of Pantulf.

Philip (Sheriff 1633) was ſon of Thomas, 3rd ſon of Thomas (Sheriff 1567), who was 4th from Nicholas (Sheriff 1440), grandſon of Humphrey, the brother of John (Sheriff 1394).

Her. Vis. Eyton. Blakeway.

Pr. Rep.: Thomas Campbell Eyton, Eſq., of Eyton.

Fewtrell.—Per chev. arg. and ſa., three mullets counter-changed, on a chief of the laſt as many leopards' faces of the firſt. Creſt: A leopard's head ppr., gorged with a collar arg., charged with three mullets ſa.

Confirmed to Richard Fewtrell, of Downe, 3rd in deſcent from John Fewtrell, of the ſame place. *Her. Vis. 1623.*

Fisher.—Per bend or. and gu. (another—gu. and or.), a griffin ſegreant counterchanged, within a border vair. Creſt: On the trunk of a tree lying feſſways, a branch ſprouting from the dexter end, and thereon a honey-ſuckle ppr., a kingfiſher alſo ppr., holding in his beak a fiſh or.

Confirmed to Richard Fiſher, of Ludlow, grandſon of Thomas Fiſher, of Worceſter. *Her. Vis. 1623.*

𝕱𝖑𝖊𝖙𝖈𝖍𝖊𝖗.—Sa., two poleaxes in faltire arg., ducally crowned or.

Confirmed to Thomas Fletcher, Vicar of Condover, grandfon of John Fletcher, of Denbigh. *Her. Vis.*

𝕱𝖔𝖗𝖘𝖙𝖊𝖗.—Quarterly, per fefs indented arg. and fa., in firſt and fourth quarters a bugle horn of the fecond. Creſt: A talbot paſs. arg., collared gu., lined or. nowed of the laſt.

Confirmed (with 3 quarterings) to Francis Forſter, of Watling Street, 5th in defcent from William Forſter, of the fame place, grandfon of William Forſter. *Her. Vis. 1623.*

Alſo, (with 1 quartering) to George Forſter, of Evelith, 7th in defcent from John Forſter, of the fame place. *Her. Vis.*

𝕱𝖔𝖜𝖑𝖊𝖗.—Az., on a chev. (engr.) betw. three lions paſs. guard. or., as many croffes formée (another, moline) fa. Creſt: An owl arg., ducally gorged or.

Confirmed (with 8 quarterings) to William Fowler, of Harnage Grange, 7th in defcent from John Fowler, of Foxley, Co. Bucks.
Sheriff: William, 1650. *Her. Vis. 1623. Blakeway.*

𝕱𝖔𝖝.—Arg., a chev. betw. three foxes' heads erafed gu. Creſt: A fox paſs. gu.

Confirmed (with 9 quarterings) to Sir Charles Fox, of Bromfield, grandfon of William Fox, of Ludlow, and 6th in defcent from John Fox, of Knighton, who was killed in the war againſt Glendour.
Sheriffs: Charles, 1583, 1598; Edward, 1608.
Her. Vis. 1623. Blakeway.

𝕱𝖗𝖆𝖓𝖐𝖙𝖔𝖓.—Gu., on a chev. or., three mullets fa.

Arms of Jenkin Frankton, whofe daug. Silotta m. Madock Kynaſton, Ao. 47, Edw. III. *Harl MS.*

Frere.—Sa., a chev. betw. three dolphins naiant arg.

Confirmed (with 1 quartering) to Humphrey Frere, of Charlton, 4th in defcent from Jeffrey Frere, from Co. Worcefter. *Her. Vis.*

Fylilode.—Arg., in a chief a lion pafs. guard. gu., in bafe three leopards' heads fa.

Arms of —— Fylilode, whofe daug. Katherine m. Richard Blyke, 2 Hen. VI. *Her. Vis.* 1623.

Gabbett, fee Garbed.

Gardiner.—Per fefs arg. and fa., a pale betw. three griffins' heads erafed, all counterchanged.

Confirmed (with 2 quarterings) to John Gardiner, 4th in defcent from John Gardiner, of Salop, who was 3rd from John Gardiner, Co. Lancafter. *Her. Vis.* 1623.

Garbed or Gabbett.—Gu., a griffin fegreant or., fupporting a ftandard arg., charged with an imperial eagle fa., ftaff of the third, garnifhed of the fecond.

Confirmed to Roger Garbed or Gabbett, of Righton in Condover, grandfon of Robert Garbed, of Acton Burnell, temp. Hen. VII. *Her. Vis.*

†**Gattacre.**—Quarterly gu. and erm., on the fecond and third, three piles of the firft, on a fefs az., five bezants.

Confirmed (with 2 quarterings) to William Gattacre, of Gattacre, 6th in defcent from John Gattacre, of Gattacre, temp. Hen. IV.

This John Gattacre was 6th in defcent from Stephen de Gattacre, Lord of Gattacre, temp. Hen. II. *Her. Vis.* 1623.

Pr. Rep.: Edward Lloyd Gatacre, Efq., of Gatacre Hall.

𝕲ibbons.—Paly of ſix arg. and gu., on a bend ſa., three eſcallops of the firſt.

Confirmed to Richard Gibbons, of Shrewſbury, 3rd in deſcent from Robert Gibbons. *Her. Vis.* 1623.

𝕲ough.—Sa., three nags' heads eraſed arg.

Confirmed (with 3 quarterings) to Thomas Gough, of Marſhe, 5th in deſcent from John Gough, of the ſame place, grandſon of Gruffith ap Jevan, a deſcendant of Gwenwys ap Gruffith.
Her. Vis. 1623.

𝕲ouldston.—Gu., on a feſs betw. three ſaltires arg., an annulet ſa.

Confirmed to Francis Gouldſton, 6th in deſcent from Philip Gouldſton, ſon of Francis Gouldſton, of Gouldſton. *Her. Vis.*

𝕲regory.—Per pale arg. and az., two lions ramp. endorſed and counterchanged. Creſt: Two lions' heads endorſed and conjoined arg. and az., collared or.

Confirmed (with 2 quarterings) to John Gregory, of Rodington, ſon of Gilbert Gregory, of Rodington and Mancheſter, who was 3rd in deſcent from Adam Gregory, of Highurſt, Co. Lancaſter.
Her. Vis. 1623.

𝕲rey.—Gu., a lion ramp. within a border engr. arg. Creſt: A ram's head arg.

The arms of Edward Grey, Lord Powis, 5th in deſcent from Sir John Grey, Lord Powys, who m. Johanna, d. and co-h. of Edward Charlton, Lord of Powis.

Sheriff: John, 1257. *Her. Vis. Blakeway.*

Guttyns.—Gu., on a fefs betw. three goats' heads erafed arg., as many pellets.

Confirmed to Thomas Guttyns, 9th in defcent from Thomas Guttyns, who was fon of Rees ap Guttyn. *Her. Vis.*

Hall.—Gu., a wyvern or., within a border az., charged with an enurny of eight lions, and a verdoy of as many fleurs-de-lis of the fecond. Creft: On the ftump of a tree couped or., a wyvern with wings endorfed fa., guttée d'or, winged and lined of the firft, the line reflected over the back, grafping in his dexter claw a fword arg., hilt and pommel or.

Confirmed (with 1 quartering) to John Hall, of Northall, in Kynerfley, Ao. 16, Hen. VIII., grandfon of David Hall, of the fame place. *Her. Vis.*

Hanmer.—Arg., two lions pafs. guard. az. Creft: On a chapeau az. (gu.), turned up erm., a lion fejant guard. arg.

Confirmed (with 6 quarterings) to Jerome Hanmer, of Fenwick, 3rd in defcent from David Hanmer, of Evenall, who was 2nd fon of Richard Hanmer, of Hanmer, Co. Flint.

Her. Vis. 1623.

Hanmer.—Az., a lion pafs. guard. or.

Confirmed (with 1 quartering) as the arms of David Hanmer, of Porkington, Ao. 1589, fon of Thomas Hanmer, who was fon of Richard ap David, and defcended from Llewellyn ap Dorchogval, of Blane.

Her. Vis.

𝔥𝔞𝔯𝔩𝔢𝔶.—Or., a bend cotifed fa.

The arms of John Harley, who fignalifed himfelf at Flodden Field grandfon of John (Sheriff 1481), and 7th in defcent from Sir Robert de Harley, fon of Sir Richard (Sheriff 1301), who was 6th from Sir William, Ao. 1098, fon of Sir John de Harley.

Her. Vis. Shirley. Blakeway.

Pr. Rep.: John Harley, Efq., of Roffal.

𝔥𝔞𝔯𝔫𝔞𝔤𝔢.—Arg., fix torteaux, three, two, and one.

Confirmed (with 2 quarterings) to Edward Harnage, of Bellefwardine, 5th in defcent from William Harnage, of the fame place.

Sheriff: Hugh, 1424.   *Her. Vis.* 1623.   *Blakeway.*

Pr. Rep.: Through the female line—Sir Henry George Harnage, 3rd Baronet.

𝔥𝔞𝔯𝔯𝔦𝔫𝔤𝔱𝔬𝔫.—Sa., a fret arg., on a chief of the latter, three trefoils flipped vert. Creft: A lion's head erafed or., gorged with a collar gu., ringed, pinned, and lined arg., betw. three trefoils flipped vert.

Confirmed to John Harrington, of Bifhton, 4th in defcent from Simon Harrington, temp. Hen. VII., a fon of Simon Harrington.

Her. Vis. 1623.

†**𝔥𝔞𝔯𝔯𝔦𝔰.**—Barry of eight erm. and az., over all three annulets or. Creft: A hawk arg., beaked and belled or., preying on a pheafant of the firft.

Confirmed to Sir Thomas Harris, Bart., of Tonge Caftle, fon of John Harris, of Cruckton, who was grandfon of John Harris, of the fame place.   *Her. Vis.* 1623.

Pr. Rep.: Francis Harries, Efq., of Cruckton.

Harris.—Az., a chev. arg., betw. three hedgehogs or.

Confirmed to Richard Harris, of Abcott, grandson of Thomas Harris, of the same place.

Also to George Harris, of Stockton, 3rd in descent from John Harris, of the same place, a son of John Hill or Harris, from Co. Stafford.

Her. Vis.

Harris.—Or., three hedgehogs, two and one, az.

Arms of Sir Paul Harris, Bart., Sheriff 1637, son of Sir Thomas, of Boreatton, Sheriff 1619, who was son of Roger Harris, Draper, of Shrewsbury. *Blakeway.*

Hatton.—Az., a chev. betw. three garbs or. Crest: A hind trippant or.

Confirmed (with 9 quarterings) to Edward Hatton, of Shrewsbury, son of Thomas Hatton, of the same place, Ao. 1584, who was son of Richard Hatton, of Ellesmere, and 6th in descent from Robert Hatton, of Kistibreches, a son of Adam Hatton, of Aldersey, Co. Chester, temp. Ric. II. *Her. Vis.* 1623.

Haukeston.—Erm., a fess gu., fretty or., within a border engr. of the last.

Arms of George Haukeston, descended from Richard, Lord of Haukeston, Sheriff 1416. *Blakeway.*

Hedley.—Arg., on a bend sa., three leopards' faces or.

Confirmed to John Hedley, grandson of Richard Hedley.

Her. Vis.

Hevyn.—Az., three boars' heads couped close or., betw. nine crosses crosslet fitchée arg.

Arms of John Hevyn, of Cleobury, Sheriff 1476. *Blakeway.*

Heylin.—Sa., three nags' heads erased arg. Crest: A bear pass. sa., gorged with a collar and bell or.

Confirmed (with 5 quarterings) to Richard Heylin, of Alderton, grandson of Gruffith Heylin, of the same place, and 5th in descent from David Heylin, a descendant of Gwyn ap Helyn.   *Her. Vis.* 1623.

Heynes or **Einnes.**—Or., on a fess gu., three bezants, in chief a greyhound courant sa., collared of the second. Crest: An eagle displayed, standing on a tortoise.

Confirmed (with 5 quarterings) to Richard Heynes, of Stretton, 4th in descent from John Einnes, of Boseley, a descendant of Treffayrne, or Gwyr de Glyn, Co. Montgomery.   *Her. Vis.*

Heyward.—Gu., a lion ramp. arg., ducally crowned or.

Confirmed (with 4 quarterings) to Sir Rowland Heyward, Lord Mayor of London, Ao. 1570, son of George Heyward, of Bridgnorth.
Her. Vis.

Hibbins.—Or., a chev. embattled, guttée d'or, betw. three castles triple towered gu.

Confirmed to Thomas Hibbins, of Weo, 6th in descent from —— Hibbins, of the same place, who m. Isabel, d. and h. of William Pardy.   *Her. Vis.* 1623.

Higgons or **Higgins.**—Vert, three cranes' heads erased arg. Crest: A griffin's head erased or., gorged with a collar gu.

Confirmed (with 1 quartering) to Richard Higgons, of Shrewsbury, 5th in descent from John Higgons, of Stretton, temp. Hen. VII., a grandson of Roger Higgons.   *Her. Vis.* 1623.

Also as the arms of Richard Higgins, son of Hugh Higgins, of Stretton, and 3rd in descent from Hugh Higgins, of Boycott.
Her. Vis. 1623.

†**Hill** or **Hull.**—Erm., on a fefs fa., a caftle triple towered arg.

Confirmed to Leonard Hill, of Hill Court, fon of Humphrey Hill, and 7th in defcent from William Hill, of Hill Court, who was fon of Humphrey Hull or Hill, of Buntingfdale, and 4th from Hugh Hull, of Hull.

Alfo, (with 2 quarterings) to Rowland, fon of Humphrey Hill, of Blechley and Soulton, and 3rd in defcent from Randolph, 2nd fon of Humphrey Hill or Hull, of Buntingfdale. *Her. Vis.* 1623.

Pr. Rep.: Rowland Hill, 2nd Vifcount.

Hill or **Hull.**—Or., on a chief vert, three bulls' heads erafed of the field. Creft: On the horns of a crefcent vair or. and az., a bull's head erafed of the firft.

Confirmed to John Hill, of Silvington, fon of Henry Hill, of Bewdley, and 4th in defcent from John Hill or Hull. *Her. Vis.* 1623. *Harl MS.*

Hinde.—Arg., on a chev. az., three efcallop fhells of the field, a chief of the fecond, charged with a lion pafs. of the field. Creft: A lion's head erafed arg.

Confirmed (with 6 quarterings) to George Hinde, of Evelith, fon of John Hinde, of London. *Her. Vis.* 1623.

Hinton.—Arg., on a bend fa., three martlets of the field.

Confirmed (with 1 quartering) to Griffith Hinton, of Hinton, grand-fon of Sir Griffith de Hinton. *Harl MS.*

Hockleton.—Vert, a lion ramp. arg.

Confirmed to John Hockleton, Ao. 1589, 7th in defcent from Walter de Hockleton, 34 Hen. III., who was grandfon of Hugo de Woderton. *Her. Vis.*

𝕳𝖔𝖑𝖑𝖆𝖓𝖉.—Az., a lion ramp. guard. arg., between eleven plates, all within a border of the fecond.

Confirmed to William Holland, of Burwarton, grandfon of William Holland, of the fame place, a grandfon of William Holland.

Her. Vis. 1623.

𝕳𝖔𝖔𝖗𝖉𝖊.—Arg., on a chief or., a raven ppr. Creft: A nag's head arg., armed and maned or.

Confirmed (with 8 quarterings) to Thomas Hoorde, fon of John Hoorde, of Parke Bromage, and 10th in defcent from Richard Hoorde.

Sheriffs: Roger, 1381; Thomas, 1457, 1488.

Her. Vis. 1623. *Blakeway.*

𝕳𝖔𝖕𝖙𝖔𝖓.—Gu., betw. nine croffes pattée fitchée or., a lion ramp. of the fecond. Creft: Out of a ducal coronet or., a griffin's head arg., in the beak a bleeding hand ppr.

Confirmed (with 7 quarterings) to Richard Hopton, of Hopton, 6th in defcent from Richard Hopton, of the fame place.

Sheriffs: Roger, 1267; Walter, 1268; William, 1346; Thomas, 1430; John, 1575; William, 1591.

Her. Vis. 1623. *Blakeway.*

𝕳𝖔𝖗𝖓𝖊.—Gu., a fefs vair.

Confirmed (with 4 quarterings) to John Horne, of Little Arnold, 4th in defcent from William Horne. *Her. Vis.*

𝕳𝖔𝖘𝖎𝖊𝖗.—Per bend finifter erm. and ermines, a lion ramp. or.

Confirmed (with 5 quarterings) to George Hosier, of Cruckton, 3rd in defcent from Edward, named Hosier, of Salop, a defcendant of Tudor, eldeft fon of Rees Says. *Her. Vis.*

Houghton.—Arg., a crofs fa., in the dexter chief and finifter bafe quarters an owl ppr.

Confirmed to Roger Houghton, of Beckbury, 3rd in defcent from Roger Houghton, of the fame place, a grandfon of Roger Houghton, of Swinney. *Her. Vis.* 1623.

Huggeford.—Az., on a chev. betw. three bucks' heads caboffed, three mullets.

Arms of Sir William Huggeford, of Hugford and Middleton, Sheriff 1392. *Blakeway.*

Hull, fee **Hill.**

Humfreston.—Arg., an eagle difplayed vert, debruifed by a chev. gu., charged with three rofes of the field.

Confirmed to William Humfrefton, of Humfrefton, grandfon of William Humfrefton, of the fame place. *Her. Vis.* 1623.

Hunt.—Per pale arg. and fa., a faltire counterchanged. Creft: A lion's head erafed per pale arg. and fa., collared gu., lined and ringed or. Another—A hind's head and neck arg.

Confirmed (with 3 quarterings) to Richard Hunt, of Longnor, fon of Roger Hunt, of the fame place. *Her. Vis.* 1623.

Hussey.—Barry of fix, gu. and erm. Creft: A boot fa., fpurred or., topped erm.

Confirmed (with 13 quarterings) to Edward Huffey, of Adbrighton Huffey, 12th in defcent from John Huffey. *Her. Vis.* 1623.

𝕳𝖞𝖉𝖊.—Az., a chev. betw. three lozenges or. Creſt: An eagle ſtatant, wings endorſed ppr.

Confirmed (with 3 quarterings) to Humphrey Hyde, of Hopton Wafres, 3rd in deſcent from Richard Hyde, of the ſame place, 1500, a grandſon of Thomas Hyde, of Norbury, Co. Cheſter.

Her. Vis. 1623.

𝕴𝖓𝖌𝖑𝖊𝖋𝖎𝖊𝖑𝖉.—Barry of ſix, gu. and az., on a chief or., a lion paſs. of the ſecond.

Arms of Robert Inglefield, Sheriff 1436, ſon of Philip de Inglefield, who m. Alice, s. and co-h. of Sir John de Roſale, of the Iſle of Roſale.

Blakeway.

𝕴𝖗𝖊𝖑𝖆𝖓𝖉.—Gu., ſix fleurs-de-lis, three, two, and one, arg. Creſt: A dove arg., in the beak a ſprig of laurel vert.

Confirmed (with 11 quarterings) to Thomas Ireland, of Albrighton, 3rd in deſcent from David Ireland, of Shrewſbury, 1592, and 9th from Robert Ireland, of Oſwaldſtrye, a ſon of Adam Ireland, Co. Huntingdon.

Sheriff: Thomas, 1632.　　　*Her. Vis.* 1623.　　*Blakeway.*

𝕴𝖗𝖊𝖒𝖔𝖓𝖌𝖊𝖗.—Sa., a chev. vair or. and gu., betw. three boars' heads arg., couped of the third.

Confirmed as the arms of Iremonger.　　　*Harl MS.*

𝕵𝖊𝖓𝖓𝖊𝖓𝖘 or 𝕵𝖊𝖓𝖞𝖓𝖘.—Erm., a lion ramp. gu.

Confirmed (with 1 quartering) to William Jennens, of Wallebourne, 3rd in deſcent from Thomas Jenyns.　　*Her. Vis.*

Jenkes.—Arg., three boars' heads couped ſa., a chief indented of the laſt. Creſt: A dexter arm embowed, habited ſa., cuffed arg., enfiled with a ducal coronet or., graſping in the hand ppr., a ſword of the ſecond, hilt and pommel of the third.

Granted by Robert Cooke, Clar., to George Jenkes, of the County of Salop, gent., May 1ſt, 1582.

Confirmed to Francis Jenkes, of Wolverton, 7th in deſcent from John Jenkes, who was grandſon of Rees ap David. *Her. Vis.* 1623.

Jenyns, ſee **Jennens.**

Jerbois.—Sa., a chev. betw. three eagles diſplayed arg.

Arms of Sir Thomas Jervois, of Chelmarſh, Sheriff 1613.

Blakeway.

Jobber.—Vert, a feſs erm.

Richard Jobber, of Aſton, was 4th in deſcent from Humphrey Jobber, of the ſame place. *Her. Vis.*

Jones.—Az., a lion paſs. betw. three croſſes formée fitchée or., a chief of the laſt. Creſt: A lion ramp. or., graſping an anchor in pale ſa.

Granted by William Camden, Clar., 1610.

Confirmed to Sir Francis Jones, Lord Mayor of London 1620, ſon of John Jones, of Clareley. *Her. Vis.* 1623. *Add. MS.*

Jones.—Arg., a lion ramp. vert, (vulned in the breaſt gu.) Creſt: A ſun in ſplendour or., each ray inflamed ppr.

Confirmed to William Jones, Alderman of Shrewſbury, ob. 1612, 3rd in deſcent from Richard Jones, of Holt, Co. Denbigh.

Her. Vis. 1623.

Jorden.—Arg., a chev. betw. three greyhounds courant gu.

Confirmed to George Jorden, of Wellington, 3rd in descent from William Jorden, from Co. Lincoln.   *Her. Vis.*

Kaynton.—Arg., a pale nebulée sa.

Arms of William de Kaynton, of Coynton, Sheriff in 1346.

          Blakeway.

Kelton.—Erm., three cinquefoils in fess. sa. (pierced arg.) Crest: A lion pass. per pale erm. and ermines, ducally crowned or.

Confirmed to Arthur Kelton, grandson of Arthur Kelton, of Shrewsbury.   *Her. Vis.*

Kemsey.—Gu., three scythes in pale arg. Crest: A holly branch ppr.

Confirmed (with 1 quartering) to Richard Kemsey, 5th in descent from William Kemsey.   *Her. Vis.*

Kenwrick.—Erm., a lion ramp. sa. Crest: On a bundle of arrows lying fessways or., feathered and headed arg., bound sa., a hawk close of the second, beaked and belled of the first.

Confirmed to John Kenwrick, of Ower, 3rd in descent from William Kenwrick, temp. Hen. VIII.   *Her. Vis.* 1623.

Kerrey.—Per saltire erm. and az. Crest: A beehive sa., with bees volant or.

Confirmed (with 1 quartering) to Thomas Kerrey, of Worthen, 6th in descent from Gruffith ap David Lloyd or Kerrey, a descendant of Kadwgan, sonne of Elistan, Lord of Betton and Wye, and chief Prince of Wales.   *Her. Vis.* 1623.

Kettleby.—Arg., two chev. fa. Creft: A lion's head erafed gu.

Confirmed (with 3 quarterings) to Thomas Kettleby, of Steple, 8th in defcent from John Kettleby, from Co. Lincoln.

Her. Vis. 1623.

Kinardesley.—Gu., crufily a lion ramp. arg. Creft: On a mount vert, a greyhound fejant arg., collared or., under a holly tree ppr.

Confirmed (with 6 quarterings) to Francis Kinardefley, of Badger, 4th in defcent from Thomas Kinardefley, of Loxley, Co. Stafford, ob. 29 Hen. VIII. *Her. Vis.* 1623.

Knight.—Arg., three pales gu., within a border engr. az., on a canton of .the fecond, a fpur or. Creft: On a fpur lying feffways or., an eagle per fefs. arg. (or.) and az., wings expanded of the firft, beaked and legged gu.

Confirmed (with 3 quarterings) to Richard Knight, of Salop, 6th in defcent from Jenkyn Knight, of Salop. *Her. Vis.*

Kynaston.—Arg., a chev. engr. betw. three mullets pierced fa. Creft: An eagle's head erafed fa., ducally crowned arg., holding in its beak a trefoil flipped ppr.

Granted by Sir Gilbert Dethick, Garter, 19th April, 1569.

Confirmed, 1584, to Roger Kynafton, of Shotton, 3rd in defcent from Philip Kynafton, of Walford, fon of Griffith Kynafton, of Stokes, 22 Hen. VI., 6th from Griffith Kynafton, of the fame place, temp. Edw. I., a defcendant of Blethyn ap Kenuyn, Prince of Wales.

Roger Kynafton, Sheriff 1640, was grandfon of Roger, Sheriff 1603, and 5th from Humphrey, brother of Sir Thomas, Sheriff 1508, fon of Sir Roger, Sheriff 1462, who was 4th fon of Griffin Kynafton, of Stocks.

Her. Vis. Blakeway.

Kynaston.—Erm., a chev. gu.   Creft: A dexter arm embowed in armour, holding a fword, all ppr.

Confirmed (with 5 quarterings) 1584, to Edward Kynaſton, of Hordley, fon of Humfrey Kynaſton, of Morton, who was grandfon of Griffin Kynaſton, of Stokes, temp. Hen. VI.   *Her. Vis.   Add. MS.*

Kynaston.—Arg , a lion ramp. fa.   Creft: a lion's head erafed fa., guttée d'or.

Confirmed (with 8 quarterings) to Sir Edward Kynaſton, of Oteley, (Sheriff 1599), grandfon of George Kynaſton, of the fame place, temp. Hen. VIII., a fon of Humphrey Kynaſton, of Stokes, who was grandfon of Griffin Kynaſton, of the fame place, 22 Hen. VI.
Her. Vis. 1623.

Lacon.—Quarterly, per fefs indented erm. and az. Creft: A falcon ppr., beaked and belled or.

Confirmed (with 22 quarterings) to Sir Francis Lacon, of Kinlet, fon of Rowland Lacon, of Willey, and 5th from William Lacon, of the fame place, grandfon of William Lacon, temp. Ric. II., and 10th from Robert Lacon, of Lacon.

Sheriffs: Richard, 1415, 1477; Thomas, 1510; Richard, 1540; William, 1542; Rowland, 1571; Francis, 1612.
Her. Vis. 1623.   *Blakeway.*

Defcendant: Through the female line—William Lacon Childe, Efq., of Kinlet.

Langley.—Arg., a fefs fa., in chief three ogreffes, within a border of the fecond.   Creft: A cockatrice fa., beaked or., wattled and legged gu.

Granted by William Camden, Clar.

Confirmed to Richard Langley, of Lincoln's Inn, Town Clerk of London, fon of Roger Langley, of Shrewfbury, and grandfon of Roger Langley, of Madeley.   *Her. Vis.*

Langley.—Arg., a fefs. gu., in chief three ogreffes. Creft : On a garb lying feffways or., a dove clofe arg., (beaked) and legged gu.

Confirmed (with 3 quarterings) to Richard Langley, of Shrewfbury, fon of William Langley, of the fame place.   *Her. Vis.* 1623.

Langley.—Paly of fix arg. and vert, on a canton gu., a pheon or.   Creft : A pheon or., betw. two laurel flips vert.

Confirmed to Thomas Langley, of Brofeley, 6th in defcent from William de Langley, temp. Ric. II.   *Her. Vis.* 1623.

†Lawley.—Arg., a crofs formée extending to the extremities of the fhield, chequy or. and fa.   Creft : A wolf pafs. fa.

Confirmed (with 3 quarterings) to Sir Edward, fon of Thomas Lawley, of Wenlock, 5th in defcent from Thomas Lawley, of the fame place.

Sheriff: Francis, 1578.   *Her. Vis.* 1623.

Pr. Rep. : Beilby Richard Lawley, 2nd Baron Wenlock.

Lee.—Gu., a fefs compony or. and az., betw. eight billets arg.   Creft : On the ftem of an oak tree lying feffways fpouting out one branch fructed ppr., a fquirrel fejant, cracking an acorn, all ppr.

Confirmed (with 4 quarterings) to Sir Humphrey Lee, of Langley, 7th in defcent from Robert de la Lee, 1ft Lord of Langley, and 13th from Sir John de la Lee, temp. Edw. I., a fon of Reginald de la Lee.

Sheriffs : Robert, 1387 ; Thomas, 1395 ; Ralph, 1465 ; Richard, 1479 ; Thomas, 1547 ; Humphrey, 1600 ; Richard, 1639.

Reiner de Lea, Sheriff 1201, was fon of Hugh, and grandfon of Reginald, Sheriff 1068, and brother of Warin the Bald.

Her. Vis. Blakeway.

Lee.—Gu., a feſs counter compony or. and az., betw. ſeventeen billets, eight in chief and nine in baſe arg.

Confirmed to Lancelot Lee, of Cotton, 6th in deſcent from John Lee, of the ſame place, grandſon of Sir Thomas Lee, of Mordley, temp. Edw. III., 3rd from Sir John Lee, of Langley.   *Harl MS.*

Lee.—Arg., a feſs ſa., in chief two pellets, in baſe a martlet of the ſecond. Creſt: A talbot's head arg., collared az., to the collar a ring and line nowed of the laſt.

Granted by Sir Gilbert Dethick, Garter, 20th Dec., 1593.

Confirmed to Sir Robert Lee, Lord Mayor of London, ſon of Humphrey Lee, of Bridgnorth.   *Her. Vis.*

Lee.—(Gu.) on a croſs betw. four unicorns' heads eraſed (or.), five roundels (az.)

Confirmed to Sir Thomas Lee or Leigh, Lord Mayor of London 1558, ſon of Roger Lee or Leigh, of Wellington.   *Her. Vis.*

Leigh.—Arg., a lion ramp. gu. Creſt: A demi-lion ramp. gu.

Confirmed to Thomas Leigh, ſon of John Leigh, of Elmer, deſcended from Leigh, of High Lee.   *Her. Vis.* 1623.

Leigh, ſee **Lee.**

*Leighton.—Quarterly per feſs indented or. and gu. Creſt: A wyvern, wings expanded ſa.

Confirmed (with 11 quarterings) to Robert Leighton, of Watleſburgh, 5th in deſcent from John Leighton, of the ſame place (Sheriff 1468), who m. Anchoret, d. and co-h. of Sir John de Burgh, and 15th from Sir Titus Leighton (grandſon of Totilus de Leighton, who lived before the Conqueſt).

Sheriffs: John, 1468; Thomas, 1495; Edward, 1568, 1588.

            Her. Vis. 1623. *Blakeway.*

Pr. Rep.: Sir Baldwin Leighton, 7th Baronet.

Le Strange.—Gu., two lions pass. in pale arg.

Arms of Le Strange, Lords of Knockin.

Sheriffs : Guy, 1160; John, 1237; John, 1309.   *Blakeway.*

Leveson.—Az., three holly leaves or.   Crest : A goat's head erased erm., attired or.

Confirmed (with 6 quarterings) to Sir Walter Leveson, of Lilleshall (Sheriff 1576), grandson of James Leveson, of the same place, 3rd son of Richard Leveson, of Prestwood, who was son of Richard Leveson, of Willnall, 44 Edw. III., and 5th from Richard Leveson.

         ,   *Harl MS.*

Lewis.—Gu., a griffin segreant or.   Crest : A demi-griffin or.

Confirmed (with 1 quartering) to Edward Lewis, of Sutton, grandson of Edward Lewis, of Broughton.   *Harl MS.*

Lewis.—Erm., a lion ramp. within a border az.

Confirmed to Thomas Lewis, grandson of Lewis ap Evan Coytmore, a descendant of Hova Grigg ap Sandiff ap Elider.   *Her. Vis.*

Lingayne or Lingen.—Barry of six or. and az., on a bend gu. (az.), three roses arg.   Crest : Out of a ducal coronet or.,a bundle of leeks stems vert, headed arg.

Confirmed (with 1 quartering) to Francis Lingayne, of Caure, grandson of William Lingayne, from Co. Hereford.   *Her. Vis.*

Lister.—Erm., on a fess sa., three mullets arg.   Crest : A stag's head erased ppr.

Confirmed (with 3 quarterings) to Richard Lister, of Rowton, 4th in descent from Richard Lister, of the same place, son of William Lister, of Shrewsbury.   *Her. Vis.* 1623.

Lloyd.—Arg., an eagle diſplayed with two heads ſa., beaked gu. Creſt: A ſtag's head eraſed ppr., attired or.

Confirmed (with 11 quarterings) to John Lloyd, 3rd in deſcent from Robert Lloyd, of Llwynymaon, a deſcendant of Blethen Vaughan.

Her. Vis.

Lloyd.—Sa., three horſes' heads eraſed arg. Creſt: A horſe's head eraſed arg.

Confirmed (with 7 quarterings) to Priam Lloyd, of Marington, 4th in deſcent from David Lloyd, ſon of Sir Griffith Vaughan, who was 4th from Kadwgan Wentwith. *Her. Vis.* 1623.

Lloyd.—Gu., a lion ramp. reguard. or.

Confirmed (with 1 quartering) to Samuel Lloyd, of Ludlow, ſon of Evan Lloyd, of Bryn-y-coed, Co. Brecknock, who m. Elizabeth, d. and h. of Thomas Huett. *Her. Vis.* 1623.

Lockyer.—A lion ramp. arg., maned or., collared ſa.

Confirmed to Francis Lockyer, of Wenlock, 3rd in deſcent from William Lockyer, of the ſame place, 1498. *Her. Vis.* 1623.

Lowe.—Gu., a wolf ſtatant arg. Creſt: An ermine paſs. ppr., collared or., lined and ringed gu.

Granted by Robert Cooke, Clar., Ao. 1586, to William Lowe, of Shroſebury.

Confirmed to Thomas Lowe, of Highley, grandſon of William Lowe, of the ſame place.

Sheriff: Humphrey, 1439.

Her. Vis. 1623. *Queen's Coll. MS. Blakeway.*

Ludlowe.—Arg., a lion ramp. ſa., vulned all over gu.

Confirmed to Humfrey Ludlowe, 12th in deſcent from Laurence Ludlowe, whoſe d. and h. Elizabeth m. Humphrey Hill, of Hill's Court.

Sheriffs: John, 1360 &c.; William, 1417 &c.; Sir Richard, 1478.

Her. Vis. Blakeway.

Lutteley.—Quarterly, or. and az., four lions ramp. counterchanged.

Confirmed (with 3 quarterings) to John Lutteley, of Bromcroft, grandſon of John Lutley, of Coſton, and 9th from William Lutley, of Munſlow Hall. *Her. Vis.* 1623.

Luttley.—Same arms as preceding.

Confirmed (with 2 quarterings) to John Luttley, 6th in deſcent from John Luttley, of Luttley. *Harl MS.*

Lutwich.—Or., a tiger paſs. gu. Creſt: A tiger's head eraſed gu., tufted and maned or.

Confirmed to Edward Lutwich, of Lutwich, 5th in deſcent from Thomas Lutwich, of the ſame place, and 11th from Roger, Lord of Lutwich. *Her. Vis.* 1623.

Lyster, ſee Liſter.

Mackworth.—Per pale indented ſa. and erm., on a chev. gu., five croſſes pattée or. Creſt: A cock gu. (beaked, legged, combed, and wattled or.)

Confirmed to John Mackworth, of Salop, 3rd in deſcent from John Mackworth. *Harl MS.*

Madocks.—Per pale gu. and az., two lions paſs. or. Creſt: A lion ſejant or., in the dexter paw a ſword arg., hilt and pommel of the firſt.

Arms of Nicholas Madocks, whoſe d. and co-h. Joana, m. Richard Ward. *Her. Vis.*

Manwaring.—Arg., two bars gu.   Crest : Out of a ducal
   coronet or., an aſs' head in a hempen halter ppr.

Confirmed to Arthur Manwaring, of Ightfield, 6th in deſcent from
William Manwaring, of the ſame place, temp. Hen. VII.

Sheriffs : George, 1505; Richard, 1532; Arthur, 1563, 1577.

Her. Vis.   Blakeway.

Marston.—Sa., a chev. indented erm.

Confirmed to Edward Marſton, of Aſtcot, 5th in deſcent from John
Marſton, of the ſame place, and 9th from Robert de Maiſton, of
Marſton, Co. Lincoln, temp. Edw. I.   *Harl MS.*

Marston.—Sa., a feſs dancettée erm., betw. three fleurs-
   de-lis arg.   Creſt : A demi-greyhound ſa., gorged
   with a collar dancettée erm.

Confirmed to Richard Marſton, of Heyton, deſcended from Marſton,
of Marſton.   *Her. Vis.* 1623.

Mason.—Or. (vert), two lions combatant ſa. (or.)

Confirmed to Edward Maſon, of Diddleſbury, grandſon of Richard
Maſon, temp. Hen. VII., who was 3rd from Richard le Maſon, temp.
Ric. II.   *Harl MS.*

Mavison.—Az., a chev. engr. betw. three mullets ſa.

Confirmed to Adam Maviſon, of Berwick, (5th in deſcent from
Adam Maviſon, of Maviſon,) whoſe d. and h. Edith m. Thomas
Wydcombe, Co. Somerſet.   *Her. Vis.*

Meire.—Arg., a ſhip ſa.   Creſt : A mermaid ppr.,
   crined or.

Confirmed (with 3 quarterings) to John Meire, of Bowbridge and of
Claverley, 2nd ſon of John Meire, of Meire, Co. Cheſter.

Her. Vis. 1623.

Meredith.—A lion ramp. ſa., over all a bend finiſter or.

Confirmed (with 5 quarterings) to Hugh Meredith, of Oſweſtry, 1584, ſon of Thomas Meredith, of Abertanat, a deſcendant of Ennyon, Lord of Abertanat. *Harl MS.*

Midleton.—Arg., on a bend vert, three wolves' heads eraſed of the field. Creſt: A wolf's head eraſed ppr.

Confirmed (with 5 quarterings) to Rowland Midleton, of Midleton, 6th in deſcent from Philip Midleton, ſon of Reryd ap David de Gwyth, who m. Cecilia, d. and h. of Sir Alexander Midleton, of Midleton, which Alexander was 4th from Thomas Midleton, of the ſame place. *Her. Vis.* 1623.

Millington, ſee **Singe.**

Mitton,—Per pale az. and gu., an eagle diſplayed with two heads or.

Confirmed (with 7 quarterings) to Richard Mitton (Sheriff 1610), great-grandſon of Richard (Sheriff 1544), and 10th from Philip Mitton, who was ſon of Owen Mitton, of Wilts, the grandſon of Roger Mitton, of the ſame County. *Harl MS. Blakeway.*

Mitton.—Arg., a cinquefoil az.

Arms of Thomas Mitton, of Halſton, Parliamentary Sheriff 1645, and Knight of the Shire 1654; he was ſon of Richard Mitton, Sheriff 1610.

John Mitton, of Weſton, who died 1532, 3rd in deſcent from Richard Mitton, bore as his arms—Arg., an eagle diſplayed with two heads within a border engr. or. *Her. Vis. Blakeway.*

Modlicott.—Sa., a lion ramp. arg.

Confirmed to Thomas Modlicott, of Harwood, ſon of Thomas Modlicott, and 9th from Llewelyn de Modlecott. *Harl MS.*

Moore or More.—Sa., a swan close arg. (ppr., beaked gu.), within a border engr. or. (arg.) Crest: An eagle arg., preying on a hare sa.

Granted by William Harvey, Clar., 1561, to Thomas Moore, of Larden.

Confirmed to Jasper Moore, of Larden, 5th in descent from Richard Moore (ob. 1434), of the same place, who was son of William Moore, (temp. Ric. II.)

(This William Moore was probably a descendant of Sir Roger de la More, temp. Edw. III., the cousin of Thomas de Mora, companion of Edward the Second in Berkeley Castle, and descended from Richard de Mora, temp. John. The before-named Jasper Moore was cousin to Richard Moore, Sheriff 1619, and who represented Bishops Castle in the Long Parliament, whose son Samuel took a leading part in the civil commotions of the time, and gallantly defended, for the Parliament, Hopton Castle, during a month's siege, with only thirty-one men, against an attacking force of five hundred horse and foot.)   *Harl MS. Fam. Doc.*

Sheriff: John de la More, 1366.   *Blakeway.*

Pr. Rep.: Rev. Thomas Frederick More, of Linley Hall.

Moore.—Per pale az. and arg., barry of twelve counter-changed.

Confirmed to Charles Moore, of the Moore, 9th in descent from Sir Robert de la Moore.   *Her. Vis.*

Morton.—Arg., a chev. betw. three trefoils slipped sa. Crest: A cock's head holding in the beak a trefoil slipped or., betw. two wings az., wattled and collared gu.

Granted by Robert Barker, Garter, to Richard Morton, of Houghton, 28 Hen. VIII.

Confirmed (with 5 quarterings) to Robert Morton, of Houghton, son of Richard Morton.   *Her. Vis.*

Montgomery.—Gu., a chev. arg., betw. three fleurs-de-lis or. Another—Or., an eagle difplayed az., beaked and armed gu.

Confirmed to Richard Montgomery, 3rd in defcent from John Montgomery, of Shrewfbury, who was 5th from Baldwine Montgomery.

Her. Vis.

Montgomery.—Az., a lion ramp. within a border or.

The arms of Roger de Montgomery. *Her. Vis.*

Mynd.—Az., on a chev. gu., betw. three lions' heads erafed fa., as many bees volant. Creft: A heath-cock arg.

Confirmed (with 1 quartering) to Thomas, fon of William Mynd, of Mynd, and 9th in defcent from Sir Symon Mynd, of the fame place.

Her. Vis.

Mytton, fee **Mitton.**

Nedham.—Arg., a bend engr. az., betw. two ftags' heads caboffed fa. (a canton or.) Creft: In flames, a phœnix rifing, all ppr.

Confirmed (with 11 quarterings) to Robert Nedham, of Shenton (Sheriff 1607), fon of Sir Robert (Sheriff 1565), and grandfon of Sir Robert, of the fame place (Sheriff 1529), and 7th from William Nedham, temp. Edw. III., a grandfon of John Nedham, of Nedham, Co. Derby, 4 Edw. III. *Harl MS. Blakeway.*

Pr. Rep: Francis Jack, 2nd Earl of Kilmore.

Newport.—Arg., a chev. gu., betw. three leopards' faces ſa.
   Creſt: An unicorn's head eraſed arg., armed, crined,
   and ducally gorged or.

Confirmed (with 17 quarterings) to Sir Richard Newport, of High
Ercall (Sheriff 1628, and created Lord Newport, 1642), ſon of Sir
Francis Newport (Sheriff 1586), and grandſon of Sir Richard (Sheriff
1552), who was ſon of Thomas (Sheriff 1550), and 3rd from William
(Sheriff 1473), and 5th from Thomas, of High Ercall (Sheriff 1404),
and 9th from Henry de Newport.   *Her. Vis.* 1623.   *Blakeway.*

Pr. Rep.: Through the female line—Orlando George Charles,
3rd Earl of Bradford.

Newton.—Arg., a croſs ſa., jeſſant-de-lis or.   Creſt: A
   ſerpent entwined round an eagle's leg eraſed at the
   thigh ppr.

Confirmed to Peter Newton, grandſon of John Newton, of Highlee,
and 6th from Sir John Newton, of Beverley.

Sheriffs: Peter, 1503; Francis, 1602; John, 1635.
                            Her. Vis. 1623.   *Blakeway.*

Niccolls.—Sa., a pheon arg., the point downwards.

Arms of Thomas Niccolls, of Shrewſbury, Sheriff 1641, ſon of John
Niccolls, Bailiff of the town 1608.   *Blakeway.*

Deſcendant: William H. Niccolls, Eſq., of Newnham.

Normicot or **Normicote.**—Sa., a feſs or., betw. three
   eſcallop ſhells arg.

Confirmed (with 3 quarterings) to John Normicote, of Corſton,
grandſon of William Normicot, of the ſame place.   *Her. Vis.* 1623.

Norton.—Or., two bars gu., on a chief az., an ineſcutcheon
   erm.

Arms of Bonham Norton, Sheriff 1611.   *Blakeway.*

Ockley or **Okeley.**—Arg., on a fefs betw. three crefcents gu., as many fleurs-de-lis or.

Confirmed to Richard Ockley, 8th in defcent from John Ockley, of Ockley. *Her. Vis.*

Onneslow or **Onslow.**—Arg., a fefs gu., betw. fix Cornifh choughs ppr. Creft . A falcon fa., legged and billed or., preying on a partridge of the laft.

Confirmed (with 1 quartering) to Richard Onneflow, of Onneflow, Ao. 1584, 7th in defcent from Thomas de Onflow, 10 Edw. II., who was grandfon of Roger Onflow.

Sheriff: Humphrey, 1566. *Her. Vis. Blakeway.*

Oteley.—Arg., on a bend az., three oat fheaves or. Creft : An oat fheaf or., banded vert.

Confirmed (with 1 quartering) to Thomas Oteley, of Pitchford, 4th in defcent from Thomas Oteley, of the fame place, who was grand-fon of George Oteley, of Oteley.

Sheriffs : William, 1500; Francis, 1645.
Her. Vis. 1623. Blakeway.

Owen.—Arg., a lion ramp. and a canton fa. Creft: Two eagles' heads conjoined and erafed per fefs or. and gu. (membered of the laft.)

Confirmed (with 13 quarterings) as the arms of Sir William Owen, of Shrewfbury, 3rd in defcent from Owen ap Gruffith, a defcendant of Edwin, Lord of Engleford, Ao. 1075.

Alfo to Sir Roger Owen, of Condover (Sheriff 1604), grandfon of Richard Owen, of Salop, 2nd fon of Owen, fon of Gruffith.

Sheriffs: Robert, 1618; William, 1623. *Her. Vis. Blakeway.*

Defcendant : Through the female line—Reginald Cholmondeley, Efq., of Condover.

𝕺𝖜𝖊𝖓.—Vert, a chev. betw. three wolves' heads erafed arg. Creft: A wolf paffant arg.

Confirmed (with 5 quartering*) to Robert Owen, of Shrewfbury, 4th in defcent from Owen ap Evan, a defcendant of Reridd Vlaidd, Lord of Brynn, Ao. 1108.   *Her. Vis.* 1623.

𝕺𝖜𝖊𝖓.—Or., a lion ramp. gu. Creft: A griffin's head gu., betw. two wings or.

Confirmed (with 5 quarterings) to Edward Owen, of Adbrightley, grandfon of David ap Owen, of Salop, a fon of Owen Keifeilock.
                            Her. Vis. 1623.

𝕻𝖆𝖗𝖆𝖒𝖔𝖗𝖊.—Arg., on a fefs az., three crefcents of the field. Creft: An antelope fejant or., attired, maned, and langued fa.

Confirmed to Richard Paramore, of Wildertop, fon of John Paramore, of Shipton.   *Her. Vis.*

𝕻𝖆𝖗𝖙𝖞𝖓 or 𝕻𝖊𝖗𝖙𝖞𝖓.—Vert, a lion ramp. holding in his forepaws a halbert erect arg.

Confirmed (with 1 quartering) to John Partyn, grandfon of Richard Partyn, of Staffordfhire.   *Her. Vis.*

𝕻𝖆𝖚𝖑𝖊 or 𝕻𝖆𝖜𝖑𝖊.—Arg., two bars az., a canton fa. Creft: A garb vert, banded or.

Confirmed to Francis Paule, brother of Sir George Paule, of Lambeth, and grandfon of John Pawle.   *Her. Vis.*

𝕻𝖊𝖒𝖇𝖗𝖎𝖉𝖌𝖊.—Or., three bars az.

Confirmed to Sir Walter Pembridge, 7th in defcent from Sir Henry Pembridge, a fon of Ralph Pembridge.   *Her. Vis.*

Peryns.—Arg., on a fefs fa., three leopards' faces of the field, betw. three pine apples vert. Creft: A pine apple or., ftalked and leaved vert.

Confirmed to Roger Peryns, of Brockton, grandfon of Peter Peryns, of Charnock Hall, Co. Derby. *Her. Vis.*

Peshale.—Arg., a crofs flory formée fa., on a canton gu., a wolf's head erafed of the field.

Arms of Sir Richard de Pefhale, of Chetwynd (Sheriff 1333.)

Blakeway.

Phillips.—Arg., a crofs flory, engr. fa., betw. four Cornifh choughs ppr. Creft: The trunk of a tree lying fefs-ways, and fprouting at the dexter end vert, thereon a Cornifh chough ppr.

Confirmed to Edward Phillips, of Shrewfbury, 3rd in defcent from John Phillips, of Kaerfows and Shrewfbury. *Her. Vis.*

Phillips.—Or., on a chev. gu., three cocks' heads erafed arg. (combed and wattled of the firft.)

Confirmed to Francis Phillips, of Chelmick, 3rd in defcent from —— Phillips, of the fame place. *Her. Vis.*

Phillips.—Arg., three cinquefoils (trefoils) in pale betw. two flaunches vert. Creft: A horfe pafs. erminois, gorged with a chaplet of laurel vert.

Confirmed to Thomas Phillips, of Netley, 3rd in defcent from Richard Phillips, a younger brother, of Picton, Co. Pembroke.

Her. Vis.

Philpot.—Gu., a fefs or., betw. three fwans clofe arg.

Confirmed (with 2 quarterings) to Richard Philpot, of Salop, fon of Rees Philpot, of Hereford. *Her. Vis.*

Piard.—A lion ramp.

Confirmed as the arms of John Piard, of Northbury, grandfon of Roger Piard, temp. Hen. IV.   *Her. Vis.*

Pichford.—Az., a cinquefoil betw. fix martlets or.   Creft: An oftrich arg., beaked and ducally gorged or.

Confirmed as the arms of —— Pichford.   *Harl MS.*

Pierrepoint.—Arg., femée of cinquefoils gu., a lion ramp. fa., with crefcent for difference.

Arms of William Pierrepoint, of Tong Caftle, Sheriff 1638.
                                                                    Blakeway.

†**Pigott.**—Erm., three fufils in fefs fa.

Confirmed (with 8 quarterings) to Robert Pigott, 4th in defcent from William Pigott, of Willafton.

Alfo as the arms of Peter Pigott, of Willafton, temp. Edw. I., 4th from William Bigot, a grandfon of Humphrey Bigot, Lord of Willafton and the Marches of Wales. The before-named Peter left two daughters, co-h. Johanna m. John Corbett, and Petronilla m. Hugh Paunton.

Alfo the lineage of Walter Pigott, fon of Thomas Pigott, of Chetwyne, who was 3rd in defcent from Robert Pigott, of the fame place.

Sheriffs: Robert, 1517, 1574; Thomas, 1615; Walter, 1624.
                                                   Her. Vis.   Blakeway.
Pr. Rep.: Rev. John Dryden Piggott-Corbet, Sundorne Caftle.

Pitt.—Barry of fix or. and az., on a chief of the fecond, three eftoiles pierced of the firft.   Creft: A dove with wings expanded arg., beaked and legged gu., betw. two ears of wheat or.

Confirmed (with 3 quarterings) to James Pitt, of Curewyard, 3rd in defcent from John Pitt, of the fame place, a fon of Robert, who m. Jane, d. and h. of Thomas de la Poole.   *Her. Vis.*

†**Plowden.**—Az., a fefs dancettée, the two upper points terminating in fleurs-de-lis or. Another—Az., a fefs dancettée betw. three fleurs-de-lis or.

Confirmed to Humphrey Plowden, fon of John Plowden, of Plowden, and 8th in defcent from Roger Plowden, of the fame place, faid to have been at the Siege of Acre with Ric. I.

Alfo to Edmund Plowden (fon of Humphrey), a famous lawyer.

Harl MS.   Shirley.

Pr. Rep.: William Henry Francis Plowden, Efq., of Plowden.

Pontesbury.—Sa., on a fefs betw. three martlets or., as many fleurs-de-lis az.

Confirmed to Thomas Pontefbury, 4th in defcent from Thomas Pontefbury.   *Her. Vis.*

Pope.—Or., two chev. gu., a canton az.   Creft: A cubit arm erect, habited gu., cuffed erm., holding in the hand ppr., a pair of fcales or.

Granted by Sir Gilbert Dethick, Garter, to Roger Pope, of Shrewsbury, and his brothers Robert and Richard.

Confirmed to Roger Pope, of Shrewfbury, grandfon of the beforenamed Roger, and 5th from John Pope, of Guilsfield, Co. Montgomery.

Her. Vis. 1623.

Powell.—Arg., three boars' heads couped fa.

Confirmed (with 1 quartering) to Richard Powell, of Worthen, fon of Richard Powell, Alderman of Shrewfbury, 4th from Howell ap Ithell, of Henllen, Co. Denbigh.

Sheriffs: Thomas, 1573; Robert, 1594, 1647.

Her. Vis. 1623.   *Blakeway.*

Poyner.—Or., a parrot clofe vert. Creft: A demi-buck ppr., attired or., holding in his feet a chaplet of laurel vert, charged on the fhoulder with a bugle horn ftringed or.

Confirmed to William Poyner, of Shrewfbury, 6th in defcent from William Poyner, of Bedeflowe, fon of William Poyner.　*Her. Vis.*

Prince.—Gu., a faltire or., furmounted of a crofs engr. erm. Creft: Out of a ducal coronet or., a cubit arm, habited gu., cuffed erm., holding in the hand ppr., three pine apples of the firft, ftalked and leaved vert.

Granted to Richard Prince, of the Abbey Foregate, by Robert Cooke, Clar.

Confirmed to his fon, Sir Richard (Sheriff 1627, and who built the Whitehall), and who was 4th in defcent from John Prince, of Salop.
　　　　　　　Her. Vis. Qu. Coll. MS. Blakeway.

Proude.—Or., on a chev. gu., three bars fa. Creft: A crofs formée fitchée or., charged with three (five) pellets, a chaplet of laurel entwined round the crofs vert.

Confirmed as the arms of Proude.　　　　　*Harl. MS.*

Purcell.—Barry nebulée of fix arg. and gu., on a bend fa., three boars' heads couped clofe of the firft. Creft: A boar's head erafed clofe arg.

Confirmed (with 4 quarterings) to Edward Purcell, of Onneflow, 7th in defcent from Richard Purcell, of Marton, who m. Margaret, d. and h. of Richard Purcell, of Onneflow.

The before-named Richard Purcell, of Marton, being grandfon of Richard, 2nd fon of John Purcell, of Onneflow, and 5th in defcent from William Purcell, of Marton and Winfbury.　*Her. Vis.*

Purslowe.—Arg., a crofs flory engr. fa., within a border engr. gu., bezantée.   Creft : A hare fejant erm.

Confirmed (with 4 quarterings) to Robert Purflowe, of Sudbury, 5th in defcent from William Purflowe, who m. Eleanor, d. and co-h. of John Eyton, of Eyton and Marfh, temp. Ric. II.

Sheriff : Robert, 1609.   *Her. Vis.   Blakeway.*

Pyrs.—Quarterly or. and az., in each quarter a pheon counterchanged.

Confirmed to William Pyrs, of Shrewfbury, grandfon of Richard Pyrs.   *Her. Vis.*

Richardson.—Arg., three chaplets vert.

Confirmed (with 1 quartering) to Jofhua Richardfon, of Broughton, fon of Thomas Richardfon, of Whitchurch, who m. Maria, d. and h. of Thomas Ridley, of Broughton.   *Her. Vis.* 1623.   *Harl MS.*

Ridley.—Gu., a chev. arg., betw. three hawks clofe or.   Creft : A greyhound pafs. arg., collared gu.

Confirmed to Richard Ridley, Ao. 1592, fon of Lancelott Ridley, of Bowlding, who was grandfon of Lancelott Ridley.   *Her. Vis.*

Ridley.—Arg., on a mount vert, a bull ftanding gu., armed or.

Confirmed to Thomas Ridley, of Broughton, grandfon of Ralph Ridley, of Alkington, who was fon of Hugh Ridley, of Ridley, Co. Chefter.

Maria, d. and co-h. of Thomas Ridley, of Broughton, m. Thomas Richardfon, of Whitchurch.   *Her. Vis.* 1623.

Ridgley.—Arg., on a chev. fa., three mullets pierced of the firft.   Creft : A buck's head erafed or.

Confirmed to Francis Ridgley, of Albright Huffey, fon of Humphrey Ridgley, of Longdon, Co. Stafford.   *Her. Vis.*

Roberts.—Or., a fess wavy, betw. three bucks trippant fa.

Confirmed as the arms of Roberts.   *Harl MS.*

Rocke.—Or., three chefs rooks, and a chief embattled fa. Creft: On a rock ppr., a martlet or.

Granted by William Camden, Clar., to Richard Rocke, of Shrewfbury. Confirmed to his fon, Richard Rocke, of the Abbey Foregate, Sheriff of Montgomeryfhire, who was 3rd in defcent from John Rocke, of Shrewfbury.   *Her. Vis.*

Pr. Rep.: John Rocke, Efq., of Clungunford.

Rogers.—Or., a fess wavy, betw. three bucks trippant fa. Creft: On a mount vert, a buck trippant fa., attired arg., ducally gorged, ringed, and lined of the laft.

Granted, 1578, by Robert Cooke, Clar., to Richard Rogers, of Little Nefs.   *Qu. Coll. MS.*

Rone.—Arg., three roebucks ppr., attired or. Creft: A buck's head erafed ppr., attired or.

Confirmed to Jerome Rone, of Longford, grandfon of Humphrey Rone. *Her. Vis.*

Rowley.—Arg., on a bend betw. two Cornifh choughs fa., three efcallops of the firft. Creft: An eftoile of eight points pierced.

Confirmed to Francis Rowley, of Wyken, grandfon of William, of the fame place.

Alfo the lineage of William Rowley, of Rowley, 3rd from George Rowley, of the fame place, fon of Robert Rowley, of Worsfield.
          Her. Vis. Harl MS.

Salter.—Gu., ten billets, four, three, two, one, or., within
a border engr. az., bezantée.   Creft: A cock's head
az., combed, beaked, and wattled gu., charged on the
neck with four billets.

Confirmed (with 3 quarterings) to Thomas Salter, of Ofweftry, 4th in
defcent from Humphrey Salter, of the fame place.

Sheriff: John, 1521.   *Her. Vis.* 1623.   *Blakeway.*

†**Sandford.**—Quarterly per fefs indented az. and erm.
Creft: A falcon with wings endorfed preying on a
▬▬▬▬▬▬▬▬▬▬▬▬

CORRIGENDA.

——

Page 59, line 8, for †**Sandford**, read *****Sandford**.
Page 59, line 19, for †**Sandford**, read *****Sandford**.

- - -- .

†**Sandford.**—Per chev. fa. and erm., in chief two boars'
heads couped clofe or.   Creft: A boar's head couped
clofe or., holding in the mouth a broken tilting
fpear az.

Granted by Robert Cooke, Clar.

Confirmed (with 1 quartering) to Humphrey Sandford, of Roffall,
5th in defcent from William Sandford, of the Ifle, who m. (Sibella)
d. and co-h. of Sir Foulke Springfeaux or Sprencheaux, of Plafh and
Donington.   The before-named William Sandford was defcended from
the Sandfords, of Sandford.   *Harl MS.* *Her. Vis.*

Pr. Rep. : Humphrey Sandford, Efq., of the Ifle.

Saye.—Quarterly or. and gu.

Confirmed to Humphrey Saye, 4th in defcent from Hugh Saye.

Her. Vis.

Scriben.—Arg., guttée de fang, a lion ramp. fa.   Creft:
A buck ppr., attired or.

Confirmed (with 3 quarterings) to Edward Scriven, of Frodefley, 4th
in defcent from John Scriven, of the fame place, temp. Hen. VI., and
8th from David Scriven.

Sheriffs : Thomas, 1497 ; Edward, 1597.

Her. Vis.   Blakeway.

Selman.—Erm., on a bend fa., three eagles difplayed or.

Confirmed (with 3 quarterings) to Thomas Selman, of Harington
Hall, grandfon of Henry Selman, of the fame place.   *Her. Vis.*

Shenton.—Az., three griffins' heads erafed or.

Confirmed to Hugh Shenton, 4th in defcent from Thomas Shenton.

Her. Vis.

Shepard or **Egerton.**—Az., on a chev. wavy or., betw.
three fleurs-de-lis arg., as many eftoiles gu.

Confirmed to Thomas Shepard, of Whettell, grandfon of John
Shepard or Egerton, of the fame place.   *Her. Vis.*

Sherar.—Arg., a fefs gu., betw. three torteaux, each
charged with a mullet or.   Creft : On a chapeau gu.,
turned up erm., a cubit arm erect, vefted az., cuff of
the fecond, holding in the hand ppr., a garb or.

Confirmed to Thomas Sherar, of Shrewfbury, 3rd in defcent from
William Sherar.   *Her. Vis.*

Singe or Millington.—Az., three mill ftones arg., two and one, each charged with a mill-rind fa. Creft: Out of a ducal coronet or., an eagle's claw arg.

Confirmed (with 1 quartering) to Richard Singe, of Bridgnorth, grandfon of Thomas Millington or Singe, of the fame place.

Her. Vis.

Slany.—Gu., a bend betw. three martlets or.

Confirmed to Sir Stephen Slany, Lord Mayor of London Ao. 1595, fon of John Slany, of Mitton, Co. Stafford. *Her. Vis.*

Smallman.—Gu., a chev. betw. three doves rifing or. Creft: An heraldic antelope fejant, holding up his dexter foot fa., armed or., gorged with a ducal coronet and lined of the laft.

Confirmed to Stephen Smallman, of Wildertop, fon of Thomas Smallman, of Elton, Co. Hereford. *Her. Vis.* 1623.

Smith.—Sa., a bend betw. fix martlets arg.

Confirmed to George Smith, of Morvill, 4th in defcent from Richard Smith, of the fame place. *Her. Vis. Harl MS.*

Smith.—Arg., on a mount vert, a lion pafs. reguard. ppr. Creft: A nag's head erafed ppr., maned fa.

Confirmed to James Smith, of Overton, 6th fon of Thomas Smith, of Crednitt, Co. Hereford. *Her. Vis.* 1623.

Spencer.—Sa., a chev. betw. three hares' heads erafed arg.

Confirmed (with 2 quarterings) to Thomas Spencer, of Whitton, 6th in defcent from Sir William Spencer, who m. Juliana, d. and h. of John de Witton. *Her. Vis.*

Sprencheaux.—Per fefs gu. and vert, a fefs and in chief a chev. conjoined arg.

The arms of Sir Foulke Sprencheaux (Sheriff 1447), of Roger (Sheriff 1279), of Edward (Sheriff 1411).

The daughters and co-h. of Sir Foulke Sprenchofe or Sprencheaux, m. William Acton, William Sandford, Sir William Leighton, and Sir Richard Lee.   *Her. Vis.* 1623. *Blakeway.*

Stanley.—Arg., on a bend az., three bucks' heads caboffed or.

Confirmed (with 5 quarterings) to Edward Stanley, of Knockinge, grandfon of Foulk Stanley, of the fame place, 3rd from Pierce Stanley, 2nd fon of Sir William Stanley, of Hotton, Co. Chefhire.

Harl MS.

Stanney.—Arg., a chev. betw. three peewits gu.

Arms of Richard Stanney, of Ofwaldftey, whofe daug. Elizabeth m. Edward Lloyd, of Llwynymaon.   *Her. Vis.*

Stedman.—Arg., a chev. gu. betw. three boars' heads couped fa.

Confirmed as the arms of Stedman.   *Harl MS.*

Stephens.—Per chev. az. and arg., in chief two falcons rifing or. Creft: A demi-eagle difplayed or., wings fa.

Confirmed to Richard Stephens, of Minfterley, 3rd in defcent from William Stephens, of the fame place.   *Her. Vis.*

Stepleton.—Az., a lion ramp. or.

Arms of John Stepleton, of Condover, Sheriff 1391. *Blakeway.*

Steventon.—Gu., a fefs arg., betw. three ftags' heads cabolfed or. Creft: A ftag's head cabolfed ppr.

Confirmed (with 2 quarterings) to William Steventon, of Dodhill, 4th in defcent from William Steventon, of the fame place, temp. Edw. IV., and 8th from Nicholas Steventon, temp. Edw. III., who was fon of Thomas Steventon. *Her. Vis.*

Stuche or **Stiche.**—Sa., three garbs or., two and one.

Confirmed to Thomas Stuche, of Stuche, 6th in defcent from William Stuche, of the fame place.

James Clyve, of Huxley, Co. Chefter, m. Katherine, d. and h. of the before-named Thomas Stuche. (See CLYVE.) *Her. Vis.*

Studley.—Gu., on a chev. arg., three croffes crofllet fitchée fa.

Confirmed to John Studley, grandfon of Thomas Studley, of the fame place. *Her. Vis.*

Sturry.—Arg., a lion ramp. purp.

Confirmed as the arms of Walter Stury, of Roffall, 5th in defcent from John Sturry, of the fame place. *Her. Vis.*

Sugdon.—Az., a fefs gu. (or.), in chief three maidens' heads couped at the fhoulders ppr., vefted and crined or., in bafe a leopard's head of the laft. Creft: A leopard's head erafed or., ducally gorged az.

Confirmed as the arms of Sugdon. *Harl MS.*

Swynnerton.—Arg., a crofs flory fa.

The arms of Humphrey Swynnerton, whofe d. and co-h. Elizabeth m. Francis Gattacre, and whofe d. and co-h. Margaret m. Henry Vernon.

John Swynnerton was Sheriff 1322, and Thomas 1342.

Her. Vis. 1623. *Blakeway.*

Syton.—Per pale az. and gu., a lion ramp. arg., betw. fourteen (eight) croffes crofflet or.

Confirmed as the arms of Syton.   *Harl MS.*

Talbot.—Gu., a lion ramp. within a border engr. or. Creft: On a chapeau gu., turned up erm., a lion pafs. or. (ftatant or., tail extended.)

Confirmed (with 35 quarterings) as the arms of John Lord Talbot, 10th Earl of Shrewfbury, 7th in defcent from John Lord Talbot Strange, of Blackmere, Furnivall, and Verdun, Governor of Anjou and Maine, Knight of the Garter, and created Earl of Shrewfbury 19 Hen VI., which Lord Talbot Strange was 9th from William Lord Talbot, who did defend Hereford for Maud the Emprefs againft King Stephen.

Sheriffs: Gilbert, 1485; John, 1528.
Her. Vis. 1623. *Blakeway.*
Pr. Rep.: Charles John, 19th Earl of Shrewfbury and Talbot..

Tanat.—Per fefs arg. and fa., a lion ramp. counterchanged.

Confirmed (with 7 quarterings) to Thomas Tanat, fon of Rice Tanat, of Abertanat, Ao. 1584, and 3rd from Jeuan Lloyd Vaughan de Abertanat, who was a defcendant of Madock ap Meredith, Prince of Powis.
Her. Vis. 1623.

Tanat.—Per bend finifter fa. and arg., a lion ramp. counterchanged, within a border engr. gu.

Confirmed to Maurice Tanat, of Blodwell, grandfon of John Tanat, of the fame place.

Jane, d. and co-h. of Maurice Tanat m. John Matthews, of Blodwell.
Her. Vis.

Thinne or **Botbille.**—Barry of ten or. and fa.   Creft: A reindeer or.

Confirmed (with 2 quarterings) to John Thinne, of Church Stretton, grandfon of Sir John Thinne, and 4th in defcent from Ralph Botville, of Church Stretton.

Sheriff: Thomas, 1634.   *Her. Vis.* 1623. *Blakeway.*

†𝕿𝖍𝖔𝖗𝖓𝖊𝖘.—Sa. (az.), a lion ramp. guard. arg. Creſt: Out of a ducal coronet or., a mermaid ppr., crined of the firſt, conjoined to a dolphin haurient of the ſame, devouring her ſiniſter hand.

Confirmed (with 2 quarterings) to Francis, grandſon of Nicholas Thornes, of Shelvock, and 8th in deſcent from Robert Thornes.

(Robert Thornes was elected Burgeſs of Shrewſbury 1357.)

Richard was Sheriff 1610.　　*Harl MS.　Shirley.　Blakeway.*

Pr. Rep.: Thomas William Thornes, Eſq.

𝕿𝖎𝖙𝖙𝖑𝖊𝖞.—Az., on a feſs betw. ſix croſſes croſſlet fitchée or., three eſcallops ſa.

Confirmed (with 1 quartering) to John Tittley, of Tittley, 7th in deſcent from Sir Thomas Tittley, of the ſame place.　　*Her. Vis.*

𝕿𝖔𝖜𝖓𝖘𝖍𝖊𝖓𝖉.—Az., a chev. erm., betw. three eſcallop ſheils arg. Creſt: A ſtag trippant arg.

Confirmed (with 7 quarterings) to Robert Townſhend, of Ludlow, grandſon of Sir Roger Townſhend, of Raynham, Co. Norfolk.

　　　　　　　　　　　　　　　Her. Vis. 1623.

𝕿𝖗𝖊𝖇𝖔𝖗.—Erm., a lion ramp. or.

The arms of Thomas Trevor, grandſon of John Trevor, of Brynn Kannalt, who died 2 Hen. VII.　　*Her. Vis.*

𝕿𝖗𝖚𝖒𝖜𝖞𝖓.—Sa., a croſs engr. or.

Arms of Roger Trumwyn, Sheriff 1308.　　*Blakeway.*

𝕿𝖗𝖚𝖘𝖘𝖊𝖑𝖑.—Arg., a fret gu., on each joint a bezant.

The arms of John Truſſell, who died 15 Hen. VII., and who was 4th in deſcent from William Truſſell.

Elizabeth, f. and h. of John Truſſell, m. John Vere, Co. Oxford.

　　　　　　　　　　　　　　　Her. Vis.

Turner.—Ermines, a crofs arg., quarter-pierced of the
field, four mill-rinds fa.

Confirmed (with 1 quartering) to Timothy Turner, of Shrewfbury,
3rd in defcent from John Turner, of Coleyhall.   *Her. Vis.* 1623.

Twiford.—Barry of four fa. and arg., on a chief gu., a
fleur-de-lis or., in a canton of the firft, a mullet of
the laft.

Confirmed to Richard Twiford, fon of Robert Twiford, of Milward,
and 4th in defcent from Richard Twiford, of Petton.   *Her. Vis.*

Vauasor.—Or., a chev. dancettée fa.

Confirmed (with 1 quartering) to John, fon of Sir Peter Vauafor, of
Spaldington, who was grandfon of John Vauafor, of the fame place.

                                                                   Her. Vis.

Vaughan.—Arg., a lion ramp. fa.   Creft: A boar's head
gu., couped or.

Confirmed (with 3 quarterings) to William Vaughan, of Dudlefton,
grandfon of Richard Vaughan, who was fon of David ap Madock, of
Dudlefton.   David ap Madock was 10th from Owen Brogyntyn, Lord
of Eduernion.   *Her. Vis.*

Veiner or **Vynor.**—Az., a bend or., on a chief arg., a faltire
engr. gu., betw. two crows ppr.   Creft: A finifter
arm embowed in armour arg., garnifhed or., holding
in the hand ppr., a ring of the fecond, mounted fa.

Confirmed to John Veiner, 3rd in defcent from Ralph Veiner, 2nd fon
of Jeuan ap Llin, of Treuailer, in Anglefey.

Alfo the lineage of Henry Vynor, of Condover, grandfon of Nicholas
Vynor, of Wiltfhire.   *Her. Vis.*

Vernon.—Arg., a fret ſa., a canton gu., quartered with (gu.) ſix annulets, three, two, and one. Creſt: A lion ramp. gu. Another—A boar's head eraſed ſa., ducally gorged or.

Confirmed (with 23 quarterings and an eſcutcheon of pretence) to Thomas Vernon, of Stokeſay, who m. Anna, d. and co-h. of John Ludlow.

Thomas Vernon, was 2nd ſon of Sir Henry Vernon, of Haddon, Co. Derby.

Sheriff: Thomas, 1524. *Her. Viſ.* 1623. *Blakeway.*

Vernon.—Same arms as preceding.

Confirmed to Sir Robert Vernon, of Hodnett, 3rd in deſcent from Humphrey Vernon, of Hodnett, 3rd ſon of Henry Vernon, of Haddon, Co. Derby. *Her. Viſ.* 1623.

Vynor, ſee **Veiner.**

†**Walcott.**—Arg., a chev. betw. three cheſs rooks ermines. Creſt: A bull's head eraſed (arg.), armed or., ducally gorged, lined, and ringed of the laſt.

Confirmed (with 1 quartering) to Charles Walcott, of Walcott, 5th in deſcent from Roger Walcott, of the ſame place, who was 4th in deſcent from Jevan Walcott, of Walcott, a deſcendant of Trahern ap Jerworth, of Gorthmoc.

Sheriff: Humphrey, 1631. *Her. Viſ.* 1623.

Pr. Rep.: Rev. Charles Walcot, of Bitterley Court.

†**Walcott.**—Arg., a croſs flory az., charged with five fleurs-de-lis or.

The arms of Sir John Walcott, of Walcott, temp. Ric. II.

Her. Viſ. 1623.

𝕎𝖆𝖑𝖑𝖔𝖕.—Arg., a bend wavy ſa.

Arms of Sir Henry Wallop, of Peynton, Sheriff 1606, who m. a
d. and co-h. of Robert Corbet, of Morton Corbet, eldeſt ſon of Sir
Andrew Corbet, Sheriff 1551.   *Blakeway.*

𝕎𝖆𝖑𝖙𝖊𝖗.—Per pale arg. and ſa., a ſaltire counterchanged,
    charged with a ſaltorel wavy of the ſame. Creſt: A
    garb or. (arg., fruɛted or.), banded gu.

Confirmed (with 3 quarterings) to John Walter, 3rd in deſcent from
John Walter.   *Her. Vis.   Harl MS.*

𝕎𝖆𝖑𝖙𝖊𝖗.—Az., a feſs indented betw. three eagles diſplayed
    arg.   Creſt: A lion's head eraſed arg.

Confirmed to Edmund Walter, of Ludlow.   *Her. Vis.* 1623.

𝕎𝖆𝖗𝖉.—Arg., two bars gu., each charged with three
    martlets or., in chief a croſs croſllet betw. two fleurs-
    de-lis az., all within a border engr. ſa.

Confirmed (with 1 quartering) to Roger Ward, of Baſchurch, 3rd in
deſcent from Thomas Ward.   *Her. Vis.*

𝕎𝖆𝖗𝖎𝖓𝖌.—Gu., on a feſs engr. or., betw. three bucks'
    heads caboſſed arg., as many bugle horns, ſans
    ſtrings ſa.   Creſt: A cubit arm ereɛt, veſted gu.
    (cuffed arg.), holding in the hand ppr., a lure of the
    firſt, garniſhed or., lined and ringed vert.

Confirmed (with 2 quarterings) to Nicholas Waring, of Shrewſbury,
5th in deſcent from Richard Waring, of the ſame place, who was ſon of
Symon Waring, of Onneſlow.   *Her. Vis.   Harl MS.*

Warram.—Erm., on a bend counter-imbattled az., three mullets or.

Confirmed to Richard Warram, of London, grandſon of Simon Warram, of Madley. *Her. Vis.*

Warren.—Chequy arg. and ſa.

Arms of Griffin Warren, of Ightfield, whoſe daug. Margaret m. William Manwaring. *Her. Vis.* 1623.

Wateis.—Or., a pale az.

Confirmed (with 3 quarterings) to Edward Wateis, of Ludlow, ſon of John Wateis, of the ſame place. *Her. Vis.* 1623.

Wattson.—Or., on a chief vert, an erm paſs. ppr. Creſt: An erm paſs. ppr. (vulned in the ſhoulder gu.)

Confirmed (with 1 quartering) to John Wattſon, of Newport, ſon of William Wattſon, of the ſame place, 4th in deſcent from Robert Wattſon, of Wattſon, Co. York. *Harl MS.*

Waverton.—Or., three eagles diſplayed, on as many ineſcutcheons ſa.

Confirmed to John Waverton, of Worsfield, 3rd in deſcent from John Waverton, of Waverton.

Jane, d. and h. of John Waverton, m. Sir George Bromley, of Cheſter. *Her. Vis.* 1623.

Weale.—Gu., a bend compony or. and az., betw. ſix creſcents arg.

Confirmed to William Weale, of Shrewſbury, 5th in deſcent from William Weale, of Cotes. *Her. Vis.*

Weaver.—Arg., two bars fa., on a canton of the laft, a garb or.

Confirmed to John Weaver, grandfon of Roger Weaver, of Tarnhall, fon of Nicholas Weaver, Co. Chefter.　　*Her. Vis.*

Weld.—Az., a fefs nebulée betw. three crefcents erm.

Confirmed (with 2 quarterings) to Sir John Weld, fon of Sir Humfrey Weld, Lord Mayor of London, ob. 1610, and grandfon of John Weld, of Eton, Chefhire.

Sheriff: John, 1642.　　*Her. Vis. Blakeway.*

Wenlock.—Gu., a chev. or., betw. three lions ramp. guard. arg.　Creft: A griffin pafs. with wings endorfed or.

Confirmed as the arms of Wenlock, of Wenlock.　　*Harl MS.*

Wheeler.—Arg., on a chief az., two Catharine wheels of the firft.　Creft: A lion's head couped arg., charged on the neck with a Catharine wheel gu.

Arms of Thomas Wheeler (who m. Elizabeth, daug. of Thomas Barnaby, of Ludlow), fon of William Wheeler, 3rd fon of Richard Wheeler, of Surrey.　　*Harl MS.*

Whitbrooke.—Gu., a lion ramp. betw. three mullets or.　Creft: A bull's head erafed arg., gorged with a ducal coronet or., armed of the laft.

Confirmed (with 5 quarterings) to Hugh Whitbrooke, of Bridgnorth, 6th in defcent from Richard Whitbrooke, of Cardington.

　　Her. Vis.

Whitbrooke.—Arg., on a chev. betw. three demi-lions ramp. az., three bulls' heads caboffed or.

Confirmed to Hugh, fon of Rowland Whitbrooke, 2nd fon of Hugh Whitbrooke, of Bridgnorth.　　*Her. Vis.*

†**Whitmore.**—Vert, fretty or., on a canton of the laſt a cinquefoil az. Crest: A cubit arm erect, veſted or., holding in the hand ppr., a roſe az., leaved and ſlipped vert, all within two wings expanded of the firſt.

Granted by Sir William Dethick, Garter, 13th November, 1593.

Alſo—Same Arms. Creſt: A falcon cloſe ſitting on the ſtump of a tree with a branch ſprouting from the dexter ſide, all ppr.

Confirmed to Sir William Whitmore, of Apley (Sheriff 1620), ſon of William Whitmore, of London, Ao. 1593, 3rd in deſcent from Thomas Whitmore, of Madeley (Claverley?).

(This Thomas was 3rd from Richard de Whytemere, of Claverley, who m. Margery, d. and h. of William Attetrall, of the ſame place, and 6th from John, Lord of Whytemere, temp. Hen. III.)

Her. Vis. Harl MS. Burke.

Pr. Rep.: Captain Thomas Charles Douglas Whitmore.

Whitton.—Or., on a chev. ſa., five bezants.

Confirmed to John Whitton, of Whitton.

Sheriffs: John, 1362; Thomas, 1407. *Her. Vis.*

Wicharley.—Per pale arg. and ſa., three eagles diſplayed counterchanged.

Confirmed to Richard Wicharley, of Wicharley, 3rd in deſcent from Roger Wicharley, of the ſame place. *Her. Vis.*

Wigmore.—Arg., three greyhounds courant ſa., collared gu.

Confirmed to William Wigmore, of Lucton, 11th in deſcent from Richard Wigmore. *Her. Vis.*

Wilcocks or **Wilkinson.**—Arg., a feſs betw. three birds'
(cocks') heads eraſed ſa.

Confirmed (with 1 quartering) to Richard Wilcocks, of Broſeley, ſon
of Rowland Wilcocks or Wilkinſon, 4th from Wilkinſon, of Denall,
Co. Cheſter.

Alſo lineage of Hugh Wilcocks, of Ponteſbury, grandſon of Thomas
Wilcocks. *Her. Vis.*

Wilkes.—Paly of eight or. and gu., on a feſs az., three
plates.

Confirmed to William Wilkes, 1592, grandſon of Thomas Wilkes.
Her. Vis.

Wilkinson, ſee **Wilcocks.**

Willaston.—Or., three mullets ſa.

Confirmed to Hugh Willaſton, 14th in deſcent from Richard, Lord
of Willaſton. *Her. Vis.*

Williams.—Sa., three horſes' heads eraſed erm. Creſt:
On a mount vert, a ſtag ſtatant arg., attired ſa.

Confirmed (with 7 quarterings) to Thomas Williams, of Willaſton,
3rd in deſcent from Reginald Williams, Sheriff of Montgomeryſhire, temp.
Hen. VIII., who was ſon of William ap David, a deſcendant of Gwenwys.
Sheriff: Thomas, 1582. *Her. Vis.* 1623. *Blakeway.*

Williams.—Or., a croſs moline betw. four lozenges az.

Confirmed to Henry Williams, of Oſwaldeſtrie, 2nd ſon of William
Meredith, a deſcendant of Guttin ap Ririd. *Her. Vis.* 1623.

Wlonkeslow.—Sa., a lion ramp. or., crowned gu., betw.
three croſſes formée fitchée arg.

The arms of Hugh Wlonkiſlow, of Wlonkiſlow, whoſe d. and h.
Iſabel m. Thomas Stuke, Lord of Stuke (ſee STUCKE). *Her. Vis.*

Wolrich.—Az., a chev. betw. three mallards arg., wings endorfed. Creft: An arm embowed in armour, holding a battle axe, all ppr.

Confirmed (with 19 quarterings) to Francis Wolrich, of Dudmafton, 6th in defcent from Roger Wolrich, of the fame place, who m. Margaret, d. and h. of Hugh Dudmafton, of Dudmafton.

The before-named Roger was 8th in defcent from Roger, Lord of Dudmafton. *Her. Vis.*

Wood.—Gu., three demi-woodmen, two and one, arg., holding clubs over their dexter fhoulders or.

Confirmed to Peter Wood, of Shinwood, grandfon of Peter Wood, of the fame place, who was fon of Alexander Wood, of Helly Hall, Co. York. *Her. Vis.* 1623.

Woodcock.—Per chev. fa. and arg., a chev. counterchanged, in chief three efcutcheons of the fecond. Creft: A pelican or., in her neft ppr., feeding her young arg.

Confirmed to Thomas Woodcock, of Newport, fon of Thurftans Woodcock, of the fame place. *Her. Vis. Harl MS.*

Wycombe or **Wydcombe.**—Paly or. and fa., three eagles difplayed, counterchanged. Creft: Out of a ducal coronet arg., a demi-eagle difplayed and collared, per pale, or. and fa., wings and collar counterchanged.

Confirmed to Francis Wycombe, of Berwick, 6th in defcent from Thomas Wydcombe, of Wydcombe, Co. Somerfet, who m. Edith, d. and h. of Adam Mavifon, of Berwick, temp. Hen. IV.
Her. Vis.

Defcendant: Rev. Philip Whitcombe, Vicar of the Abbey Church, Shrewfbury.

Wynn.—Arg., a lion ramp. ſa. Creſt: A boar's head gu., couped or.

Confirmed (with 2 quarterings) to Morgan Wynn, of Dudleſton, grandſon of John Wynn, of the ſame place, ſon of David ap Madock, a deſcendant of Owen Brogintin, Lord of Eduerneon.

Her. Viſ. 1623.

Wynnesbury.—Az., three lioncels paſs. in bend or., betw. two cotiſes gu.

John Wynneſbury, Sheriff 1492, was ſon of Sir Rowland Wynneſbury, and grandſon of Henry Wynneſbury, of Chirbury, Lord of Edgeton, and Sheriff 1391. *Blakeway.*

Wyrrall.—Gu., a chev. betw. three croſſes croſſlet arg., in chief a lion paſs. of the ſecond.

Confirmed to Sir Hugh Wyrrall, 4th in deſcent from John Wyrrall, of Greſbrook. *Her. Viſ.*

Yorke.—Az., a ſaltire arg.

Confirmed to Chriſtopher Yorke, of Ponteſbury, grandſon of John, 2nd ſon of Sir Richard Yorke. *Harl MS.*

Young.—Or. (arg.), three roſes gu. Creſt: A wolf paſs. ſa.

Confirmed (with 3 quarterings) to William, ſon of William Young, of Keynton, Sheriff 1548, who was. grandſon of Francis, 2nd ſon of Sir William Young, Sheriff 1492, and 6th from Geoffrey Young.

Harl MS. Blakeway.

APPENDIX.

Acton, Edward Farrer, Efq., of Gatacre Park, J.P. and D.L. for Cos. Salop and Stafford, Major in the Shropfhire Militia (fon of the late Edward Acton Acton, of Gatacre Park, and defcended from the 2nd fon of Sir Edward Acton, of Aldenham, who was fettled at Gatacre Park, temp. Car. II.), m. 1832 Mary Ann, daug. of the Rev. Horace Suckling, and has iffue—

Edward William Frederick, b. 1834 (who m. 1855 Helen Maria, daug. of W. P. Ranney, Efq., and has iffue one daug., Helen Beatrice).

Mary Henrietta (who m. 1859 Rev. George Ayton Whitaker, of Henftead Rectory, Suffolk).

Arms fame as Acton, of Aldenham. See page 1.

Acton, Mrs. Stackhoufe, of Acton Scott (eldeft daug. of the late Thomas Andrew Knight, of Downton Caftle), m. 1812 Thomas Pendarves Stackhoufe Acton, of Acton Scott, who died 1835, and who was repre-fentative of the old family of Acton, fettled at Acton Scott, temp. Hen. III.

Heir Pres.: Auguftus Wood, Efq., b. 1842.

Arms: Acton impaling Knight. For former fee page 2.

Atcherley, The Miffes, of College Hill Court, Shrewfbury, daugs. of the late John Atcherley, of Stanwardine, who died 1847, and who was reprefentative of the family, and defcended from Thomas Acheley or Atcherley, of Stanwardine, temp. Hen. VII., the father of Sir Roger Atcherley, Lord Mayor of London 10 Hen. VIII.

For Arms fee page 1.

Atcherley, David Francis, Efq., of Marton Hall, J.P. and D.L. for Co. Salop, Sheriff 1864, J.P. for Co. Flint (fon of the late David Francis Atcherley, and defcended through the female line from Sir Roger Atcherley, Lord Mayor of London, 10 Hen. VIII.), m. 1866 Minnie Caroline Frances Amhurft, daug. of Courtney Stacey, Efq., of Sandling, Kent, and has iffue one daughter.

Arms: Gu., on a fefs. engr. arg., betw. three griffins' heads erafed or., as many croffes pattée fitchée fa. Creft: A demi-buftard couped gu., wings elevated or., in the beak a lily arg., flipped vert.

Baxter, James, Efq., of Sibdon Caftle, J.P. and D.L. for Co. Salop (fon of the late James Fleming Baxter, of Sibdon Caftle), m. 1833 Frances, daug. of Thomas White, Efq., of Ludlow, and has furviving iffue—

Henry Fleming, b. 1838—Herbert Fleming, b. 1839.
Frances Elizabeth.

Beale, Rev. Theodore, of Hopton Caftle Rectory (fon of Thomas Beale, of Heath Houfe), m. 1863 Mary Dora, only daug. of Sir William Henry Clerke, Bart., and has iſſue—

William St. John, b. 1864—Arthur Richard, b. 1866.

Arms: Sa., on a chev. or., betw. three griffins' heads eraſed arg., as many eſtoiles gu. Creſt: An unicorn's head eraſed arg., charged on the neck with three eſtoiles gu.

Berwick.—William Noel Hill, 6th Lord Berwick, of Attingham, J.P. and D.L. for Co. Salop (2nd ſon of Richard, 4th Lord Berwick), ſuc. his brother, Richard Noel, 5th Lord, 1861.

Heir Pres. : His brother, Rev. Thomas Henry Hill, Rector of Berrington.

Arms of Hill: Erm., a feſs ſa., a caſtle with two towers arg., on a canton gu., a martlet or. Creſt: A demi-tower arg., a fawn ſtatant upon the battlements ppr., collared and chained or.

Creation, 1784.

Borough, John Charles Burton, Eſq., of Chetwynd Park and Edgmond Houſe, J.P. and D.L. for Co. Salop, Sheriff 1844, Lieut. S. Salop Yeomanry Cavalry, J.P. for Co. Stafford (ſon of the late Thomas Borough, of Hulland, Co. Derby, and deſcended from John Borrow, Sheriff of Derbyſhire 1688), m. 1848 Elizabeth Charlotte, daug. of Admiral Roberts Gawen, and has iſſue—

John Sidney Burton, b. 1852—Thomas George, b. 1857—Charles Gawen, b. 1859.

Jane Charlotte.

Arms: Gu., the root of an oak tree eradicated and couped in pale ſprouting out two branches ppr., with a ſhield of Pallas hanging thereon or. Creſt: An eagle ppr., holding the ſhield of Pallas in its claws.

𝔅𝔯𝔞𝔡𝔣𝔬𝔯𝔡.—Sir Orlando George Charles Bridgeman, 3rd
Earl of Bradford, of Weſton Park, Privy Councillor,
D.L. for Cos. Warwick and Stafford, J.P. and D.L.
for Co. Salop, Captain of S. Salop Yeomanry (ſon of
George Auguſtus Frederick Henry, 2nd Earl, and
deſcended from Sir Orlando Bridgeman, Lord Keeper
of the Great Seal, created Baronet 1660, and repre-
ſentative through the female line of the family of
Newport, Earls of Bradford, and of that of Tanat,
of Blodwell and Abertanat), ſuc. 1865, m. 1844
Selina Louiſa, daug. of Cecil, 1ſt Lord Foreſter, and
has iſſue—

George Cecil Orlando, Viſcount Newport, b. 1845—Francis Charles,
b. 1846—Gerald Orlando Manners, b. 1847.

Mabel Selina—Florence Katherine.

Creations: Baronet, 1660; Baron, 1794; Earl and Viſcount, 1815.

Arms: Sa., ten plates, four, three, two, and one, on a chief arg., a lion
paſſ. erm. Creſt: A demi-lion ramp. arg., holding betw. the paws a
garland of roſes or.

For Arms of NEWPORT ſee page 50; for TANAT ſee page 64.

𝔅𝔯𝔬𝔬𝔨𝔢, Rev. John, of Haughton Hall, late Vicar of
Shiffnal (2nd ſon of the late George Brooke, of
Haughton Hall, deſcended through the female line
from Randulf Atte-Broke, of Bobbington, Co. Stafford,
ob. 1347), ſuc. his brother George 1847, m. 1843
Georgiana Frances, daug. of John Cotes, Eſq., of
Woodcote, and has iſſue—

John Townſhend, b. 1844—Charles, b. 1846.

Arms: Chequy arg. and ſa., on a canton vert, a brock paſſ. ppr.
Creſt: A brock paſſ. ppr.

𝕭𝖗𝖔𝖚𝖌𝖍𝖙𝖔𝖓, Peter, Efq , of Tunftall Hall, J.P. and D.L. for Co. Salop, Sheriff 1839, (fon of the Rev. Peter Broughton, and defcended from Peter, brother of Sir Bryan Broughton, created Baronet 1660), m. 1818 Anne Ogilvie, daug. of John Smethwick, Efq., and has iffue—

Peter, b. 1822 (who m. 1856 Florence, daug. of Swynfen Stevins Jervis, Efq.)—John Lambart, b. 1831 (who m. Annie Selina, daug. of Ralph Adderley, Efq.)

Anna Jane—Maria Catherine Wilhelmina (who m. 1859 Ralph Thomas Adderley, Efq.)—Harriet.

Arms: Az., two bars gu., on a canton of the fecond, a crofs of the field. Creft: A fea dog's head gu., eared and finned arg.

𝕭𝖗𝖔𝖜𝖓𝖊, Thomas Browne, Efq., of Mellington Hall, J.P. and D.L. for Co. Montgomery (fon of the late Pryce Jones, of Cyfronydd), affumed 1823 the arms and name of Browne, m. 1828 Marianna Kyffin, daug. of Major Arthur Rowley Heyland, of Ballintemple, Co. Derry (who fell in command of the 40th Regt. at the Battle of Waterloo, aged 33 years), and has furviving iffue, five fons and three daughters.

𝕭𝖚𝖑𝖐𝖊𝖑𝖊𝖞-𝕺𝖜𝖊𝖓, Rev. Thomas Mainwaring Bulkeley, Vicar of Welfh Hampton and of Tedfmore Hall (2nd fon of the late Thomas Bulkeley Bulkeley-Owen, of Tedfmore Hall, and defcended through the female line from the Owens of Llunllo), fuc. his brother 1868.

Heir Pres.: His fifter, Marianne Eliza Frances, wife of the Rev. Edward Jacfon, of Thruxton, Co. Hereford.

Arms: Quarterly, 1ft and 4th arg., a crofs flory, engr. fa., betw. four Cornifh choughs ppr., on a chief az., a boar's head couped of the firft, tufked or., langued gu.; 2nd and 3rd arg., a lion ramp. and a canton fa., quartering Bulkeley.

𝕭𝖚𝖗𝖉, Edward, Efq., of Shrewfbury, M.D. and M.C. Cantab, M.R.C.S., &c., Senior Phyfician to Salop Infirmary, Surgeon to the Shropfhire Artillery Volunteers (fon of the late Henry Edward Burd, of Shrewfbury), m. 1852 Elizabeth Ellen, daug. of William Lycett, Efq., and has, with other iffue—

Edward Lycett, b. 1861.

Arms : Arg., on a fefs betw. three martlets gu., a rofe betw. two fleurs-de-lis or. Creft : An eagle's head erafed, bendy of eight arg. and fa., ducally gorged or.

𝕭𝖚𝖗𝖙𝖔𝖓, Rev. Henry, M.A., Vicar of Atcham, Rector of Upton Creffett, J.P. for Co. Salop, R.D. (fon of the late Rev. Henry Burton, Vicar of Atcham, and grandfon of Robert Lingen, who in 1748 affumed the name of Burton, and whofe father, Thomas Lingen, m. Anne, s. and h. of Thomas Burton, of Longner), m. 1845 Hon. Charlotte Belafyfe, 3rd daug. of George, 5th Vifcount Barrington.

For Arms fee Burton, of Longner, page 14.

𝕭𝖚𝖗𝖙𝖔𝖓, Rev. Robert Lingen, of Ford Houfe, and Vicar of St. Giles, Shrewfbury (fon of the late Edward Burton, of Shrewfbury, and of Llandewy, Co. Radnor, and grandfon of Robert Lingen, who in 1748, purfuant to the will of his uncle, Thomas Burton, of Longner, affumed the name of Burton), m. 1ft, 1829, Everilda, daug. of the Rev. Rigbye Baldwyn Rigbye—fhe died 1833; 2nd, 1835, Mary Ann Elizabeth, daug. of the Rev. C. Pyne-Coffin—she died 1847, leaving issue—

Edward Lingen, b. 1836 (who m. 1864 Edith Maria, daug. of C. J. T. Oakes, Esq., and died 1865, leaving issue a son, Edward)—Robert Lingen, b. 1838—Henry Lingen, b. 1840—William Blakeway, b. 1841,

Everilda Mary Ann—Mary Gertrude;

3rd, Beatrice Julia, daug. of Egerton Leigh, Esq., of High Leigh, Co. Chester.

For Arms see Burton, of Longner, page 14.

Cavendish, Henry Cavendish, Esq., of Chyknell, J.P. and D.L. for Co. Salop (son of the late Farmer Taylor, of Chyknell, Sheriff 1815, and Juliana, daug. of Richard, 2nd Lord Waterpark, assumed the name of Cavendish from his mother), m. 1862 Selina Elizabeth, daug. of the Hon. Henry Gage, and has issue—

Edith Selina—Ethel Julia—Elfrida Geraldine.

Arms: Sa., three bucks' heads cabossed arg. Crest: A snake nowed ppr.

Cheney, Edward, Esq., of Badger Hall (son of the late Lieut.-Gen. Robert Cheney, descended from Sir John Cheney, Baron Cheney, temp. Hen. VII., a descendant of Ralph de Caineto, who came to England with William the Conqueror), suc. his brother 1866.

Heir Pres.: His brother Ralph, b. 1810.

Arms: Az., six lions ramp. arg., a canton erm. Crest: A bull's scalp arg.

Childe, William Lacon, Efq., of Kinlet (only fon of the late William Childe, elder fon of Charles Baldwyn, of Aqualate, who on fucceeding to the eftate of his maternal grandfather affumed his name), fuc. 1824, m. 1807, Harriet, younger daug. of the late William Cludde, of Orleton, who died 1849, and has furviving iffue—

William Lacon, b. 1810 (who m. 1839 Barbara Dennys, daug. of Thomas Gifford, Efq., of Chillington, fhe died 1841)—Charles Orlando, b. 1812, who took in 1850 the additional name of Pemberton, under the will of the late Rev. Robert Norgrave Pemberton, of Millichope Park (and who m. 1849 Augufta Mary, 3rd daug. of the late Henry Davenport Shakefpear)—Edward George, b. 1818, Vicar of Kinlet and Cleobury Mortimer (who m. 1862 Frances Chriftina, eldeft daug. of Sir Baldwin Leighton, Bart.)—Arthur, b. 1820, Rector of Edwin Ralphe, Co. Hereford (who m. 1852 Mary Harriet, eldeft daug. of John Freeman, Efq., of Gaines, Co. Hereford.)

Harriet (who m. 1849 Rev. John Ryle Wood, Canon of Worcefter)— Anna Maria—Catherine—Lucy—Mary.

Arms: Gu., a chev. erm., betw. three eagles clofe arg. Creft: An eagle with wings expanded arg., enveloped round the neck with a fnake ppr.

For Arms of Baldwyn fee page 4.

Cholmondeley, Reginald, Efq., of Condover Hall, J.P. for Co. Salop (fon of the late Rev. Charles Cholmondeley, of Hodnet, and defcended through the female line from Sir William Owen, of Condover, Sheriff 1623, who was brother of Sir Roger Owen, Sheriff 1604, and M.P. for Shropfhire), fuc. 1864 his brother Thomas (who affumed the name of Owen), m. 1867 Hon. Alice Mary, daug. of William, 1ft Lord Egerton, of Tatton—fhe died 1868.

For Arms of Owen fee page 51.

Clubbe, see **Herbert**.

Colley, Rev. James, Vicar of St. Julian's, Shrewsbury (son of the late Thomas Colley, of Cefngwifed, Co. Montgomery), m. 1841 Sarah, d. and co-h. of the late John Brayn, of Tern Hill, and has surviving issue—

Alfred Noel, b. 1848.

Rhoda Jane (who m. 1868 the Rev. F. W. Kittermafter, Vicar of All Saints, Coventry, and has issue one son)—Sarah Elizabeth.

Arms: Three swans' heads erased arg., within a border or. Crest: An elephant's head gu., betw. two wings sa.

Cope, William, Esq., of Albrighton Hall, Barrister-at-Law (son of William Henry Cope, Esq., late of Holbeche House, Kingswinford) m. 1842 Charlotte, daug. of George Stevens, Esq., of Old Windsor Lodge, Berks, and has issue—

Herbert Ford, b. 1844—Arthur Henry, b. 1846—Edmund, b. 1848.

Alice Marion—Harriet Emily—Mary Louisa.

Arms: Arg., on a chev. az., betw. three roses gu., slipped ppr., as many fleurs-de-lis or. Crest: A fleur-de-lis or., a dragon's head issuing from the top thereof gu.

Corbet, Sir Vincent Rowland, 3rd Bart., of Acton Reynald Hall, Captain of the Shropshire Yeomanry Cavalry, J.P. for Co. Salop, and Sheriff 1862 (son of the late Sir Andrew Vincent Corbet, Bart., descended from Corbett the Norman, and Pr. Rep. of the family), fuc. 1855, m. 1854 Caroline Agnes, daug. of Admiral the Hon. Charles Orlando Bridgeman, and has iffue—

Walter Orlando, b. 1856—Gerald Vincent, b. 1868.

Alice Nina—Sybil Rachel—Ifabel Agnes—Beatrice Augufta—Judith Elizabeth—Mabel Hermione—Conftance Edith.

For Arms fee Corbett, of Morton, page 18.

Corbet, Vincent Roger, Efq., of Riverfdale, Leamington, J.P. for Co. Salop (4th fon of Sir Andrew Corbet, Bart.), m. 1838 Maria, daug. of Philip Humberfton, Efq., of Chefter, and has furviving iffue—

Robert St. John, b. 1839—Frederick Vincent, b. 1841—Everard Philip, b. 1843—Arthur Domville, b. 1847.

Charlotte Maria.

Arms fame as preceding.

Corbett, Colonel Edward, of Longnor Hall, M.P. for S. Salop, Colonel of Salop Militia (fon of the late Panton Corbett, of Longnor, and defcended through the female line from Sir Edward Corbett, Bart., 1642), fuc. 1855, m. 1842 Elizabeth Anne Therefa, daug. of Robert Scholl, Efq., of London, and has iffue—

Edward, b. 1843—Richard, b. 1844—Waties, b. 1852—Francis, b. 1854—Jofeph, b. 1862.

Therefa—Lucy—Maud—Elizabeth—Mildred—Annie—Louifa.

For Arms fee Corbett, of Longnor, page 18.

Corbett, fee **Winder**.

Curtis, Sir William, of Caynham Court, Ludlow, 3rd
Baronet, J.P. and D.L. for Co. Salop (fon of the late
Sir William Curtis, 2nd Bart.,) fuc. 1847, m. 1831
Georgina Maria, daug. of John Stratton, Efq., of
Farthinghoe Lodge, Co. Northampton, and has iffue—

William Edmund, b. 1833 (who m. Ariana Emily, daug. of Col.
W. Chefter-Mafter, of Knole Park, Gloucefterfhire, and died 1860,
leaving iffue one fon, Michael, b. 1859)—Philip Julian, b. 1838, late
H.M. 60th Royal Rifles—John Egerton, b. 1844, Lieut. in H.M. 45th
(Sherwood Forefters).

Georgina Henrietta (who m. 1868 Harry Tichborne Davenport, Efq.,
Barrifter-at-Law)—Madeline Harriet Louifa (who m. 1861 Col.
Wm. C. Chefter-Mafter, C.B.)

Arms: Paly of fix or. and az., a fefs chequy arg. and fa., on a canton
gu., a dragon's wing erect of the third, in bafe a fword ppr., pommel and
hilt of the firft, furmounting a key in faltire of the fecond. Creft:
A ram's head couped arg., furmounted by two branches of oak in
faltire ppr.

Davenport, William Sharington, Efq., of Davenport, J.P.
for Co. Salop (fon of the late Rev. Edward Sharington
Davenport, and defcended from Ormis Davenport,
Lord Davenport, temp. William the Conqueror),
m. 1835 Catherine Louifa, only daug. of S. P.
Marindin, Efq., of Chefterton, and has furviving
iffue—

Edmund Henry, b. 1839—Vivian, b. 1843—Charles Talbot, b. 1848.
Louifa Marindin.

Arms: A chev. betw. three croffes crofflet fitchée fa. Creft: A man's
head couped at the fhoulders, and fide faced ppr., with a rope round the
neck or.

Dawes, Captain Edward Alleyne, of Harnage Houfe, ferved in the 97th Regt., Light Divifion, at the Siege of Sebaftopol, has medal and clafp, and Turkifh medal (fon of the late Matthew Dawes, F.S.A., F.G.S., of Weftbrook, Co. Lancafter, and great-grandfon of Thomas Dawes, of Colefhill, Co. Warw., who m. Anna Heart, a defcendant through the female line of King Edw. I.; and maternally defcended from King Hen. III.), m. 1857 Eleanor, only daug. of J. W. Braithwaite, Efq., of Wigton, Co. Cumberland, and has furviving iffue—

Edward Wilfon, b. 1863.

Helena Willoughby—Georgina Braithwaite.

Arms : Or., on a bend engr. betw. fix battle axes erect az., three fwans with wings elevated arg., beaked and membered fa. Creft : A wyvern fa., bezantée, fupporting in its dexter claw a battle axe as in the arms.

Edwardes, Sir Henry Hope, 10th Bart., of Wootton Hall, Afhbourne, J.P. for Co. Salop, Lieut. N. Salop Yeomanry (fon of the late Sir Henry Edwardes, Bart., and defcended from Hugh Edwardes, of Kilhendre, Ao. 1549, a defcendant of Iddon, fon of Rys Sais, a powerful Britifh Chieftain), fuc. 1841.

For Arms fee page 23.

Edwards, Colonel George Rowland, of Nefs Strange (fon of the late John Edwards, and defcended from John Edwards, of Nefs Strange, temp. Car. II., who was a defcendant of Einion Efell, Ao. 1182), m. 1847

Catherine Jane, daug. of Lieut.-Gen. Edward
Armftrong, Madras Army, and has iffue—

John, b. 1850—George Rowland, b. 1852—James Murray, b. 1854—
Henry Charles, b. 1865.

Antoinette Charlotte—Catherine—Louifa Mary—Eleanor Margaret—
Eliza Henriann—Gertrude Helen—Annie Eliza Florence.

Arms : Per fefs fa. and arg., a lion ramp. counterchanged. Creft :
Within a wreath a lion ramp. as in the arms.

Egremont, Rev. Edward, Vicar of Wroxeter (fon of John
Egremont, Efq., of Reednefs Hall, and Egremont
Houfe, Yorkfhire, and defcended from the family of
Egremont mentioned in Domefday Book), m. 1824
Sara, daug. of Jacob Maude, Efq., of Sunnifide,
Co. Durham, and has furviving iffue—

Janet—Mary Louifa (who m. Captain W. N. Ruffell, R.N.)—Elizabeth
Sarah Maude (who m. Sir Henry George Harnage, Bart.)—Pauline
(who m. the Rev. Robert Steavenfon)—Arabella Ruth.

Eyton, Thomas Campbell, Efq., of Eyton and Walford
Manor, J.P. and D.L. for Co. Salop, late Captain
Rifle Volunteers, and 17 years in the Yeomanry (fon
of the late Thomas Eyton, of Eyton, and defcended
from Robert de Eyton, of Eyton (temp. Hen. II.),
fuc. 1855, m. 1835 Elizabeth Frances, d. and co-h.
of the late Robert Aglionby Slaney, of Walford
Manor, M.P. for Shrewfbury, and has iffue—

Thomas Slaney, b. 1843 (who m. 1866 Ifabel Sarah Dafhwood, daug.
of John Henry Hay Ruxton, Efq., of Broad Oak, Kent)—Robert
Henry, b. 1845—William Campbell, b. 1848.

Elizabeth Charlotte—Rofe Mary—Frances Julia—Catherine Anne—
Mary Elizabeth—Alice Emily.

For Arms and Lineage fee page 25.

𝔉𝔦𝔢𝔩𝔡, William, Esq., of Quarry House, Shrewsbury, Lieut.-Col. 1st Administrative Brigade of Shropshire and Staffordshire Artillery Volunteers (only son of the late William Field, of Longdon, Co. Stafford), m. 1838 Christiana, daug. of the late Joseph Harrison, of Birkenhead, and has issue—

William Henry, b. 1841, Captain in the 8th Hussars—Thomas Storer, b. 1850.

Mary Ann (who m. 1859 Richard Banner Oakeley, Esq., and has issue one son and one daughter).

Arms: Sa., a chev. betw. three garbs arg. Crest: A dexter arm issuing out of clouds fessways ppr., habited gu., holding in the hand also ppr., a sphere or.

𝔊𝔞𝔯𝔫𝔢𝔱𝔱-𝔅𝔬𝔱𝔣𝔦𝔢𝔩𝔡, Rev. William Bishton, of Decker Hill, J.P. for Co. Salop (son of the late Rev. William Garnett, of Haughton Hall, Co. Chester, suc. 1863 to the estates of the late Beriah Botfield, of Decker Hill, and assumed the name of Botfield), m. 1848 Sarah, daug. of William Dutton, of Haleswood House, Co. Lancaster, and has issue—

William Egerton, b. 1849—Alfred Stanton, b. 1850—Walter Dutton—Charles Ramsey.

Lucy Sophia—Grace Catharine—Annie Augusta.

Arms: Quarterly, 1st and 4th, barry of twelve per pale embattled or. and az., counterchanged, on a canton sa., a stag's attires affixed to the scalp or., for Botfield; 2nd and 3rd, bendy of four gu. and sa., a lion ramp. arg., crowned or,, a bordure indented of the last, for Garnett. Crest: Upon a rock a stag at gaze holding in the mouth an arrow fessways, all ppr.

Harley, John, Efq., of Roffall (fon of the late William Harley, Alderman of Shrewfbury, and defcended from Sir John de Harley, temp. Will. Conq.), m. Anna Maria Platt, daug. of Robert Smith, Efq., of Pontypool, and has furviving iffue—

Robert William Dacre, b. 1846, Lieut. Shropfhire Artillery Volunteers.
Anna Maria—Mary Terefa—Anne Frances Alicia.
For Arms fee page 30.

Hartley, John, Efq., of Tong Caftle, and of the Oaks, and Wheaton-Afton, Co. Stafford, J.P. and D.L. for Co. Stafford (fon of the late John Hartley, of Harborne), m. 1839 Emma, daug. of the late G. B. Thorneycroft, of Hadley Park, and Chapel Houfe, Co. Stafford, and has iffue—

George Thompfon, b. 1844, Cornet Queen's Own Royal Staffordfhire Yeomanry Cavalry—John Thorneycroft, b. 1849—Charles Albert, b. 1851.
Rofa Mary—Eleanor Jane (who m. 1868 Paynton Pigott, Efq., Barrifter-at-Law)—Alice—Conftance Emma.
Arms: Erm., on a crofs engr. gu., four quatrefoils or., in the 1ft and 4th quarters a martlet fa. Creft: Upon a mount vert, a martlet fa., in the beak a crofs pattée fitchée or.

Hazledine, John, Efq., of the Woodlands, Shrewfbury, J.P. (fon of the late William Hazledine, of Shrewfbury, Mayor 1835), m. 1827 Rhoda, d. and co-h. of the late John Brayn, of Tern Hill, and has iffue—

William St. John, b. 1834—John Rowland Lovell, b. 1843, Lieut. Shropfhire Militia (and who m. 1868 Sarah Grace Bovey, daug. of the Rev. Alfred B. Clough, Rector of Braunfton, Co. Northampton).

M

Arms: Arg., a croſs flory betw. four birds ſa., on a chief az., a pale betw. two fleurs-de-lis or., charged with the planet Mars of the ſecond. Creſt: A lion ramp. or., charged on the breaſt with a croſs flory ſa., holding in his paws a ſhield arg., charged with the planet Mars.

Herbert, Hon. Robert Charles, of Orleton, J.P. and D.L. for Co. Salop (4th ſon of Edward, 2nd Earl of Powis), m. 1854 Anna Maria, d. and h. of the late Edward Cludde, of Orleton, and has with other iſſue—

Edward William, b. 1855.

Arms: Per pale az. and gu., three lions ramp. arg.; on an eſcutcheon of pretence the arms of Cludde, for which ſee page 16.

Hill, Rowland, 2nd Viſcount Hill, of Hawkſtone, Lord Lieutenant and Cuſtos Rotulorum Co. Salop, Lieut.-Col. Commandant of the North Salopian Yeomanry (ſon of the late John Hill, eldeſt brother of 1ſt Viſcount, and deſcended from Humphrey Hill, of Adderley, to whom his uncle, Sir Rowland Hill, Kt., firſt Proteſtant Lord Mayor of London, conveyed in 1560 the Manor &c. of Hawkſtone, he being deſcended from Hugh de la Hulle, of Court of Hill, Burford, temp. Hen. III.), ſuc. the 1ſt Viſcount 1842, m. 1831 Anne, daug. of Joſeph Clegg, Eſq., of Peplow Hall, and has iſſue—

Rowland Clegg, b. 1833, J.P. and D.L. for Co. Salop—Geoffrey Richard Clegg, b. 1837, J.P. and D.L. for Co. Salop, and Major of the Shropſhire Artillery Volunteers.

Creations: Baronet, 1726; Baron, 1814 and 1816; Viſcount, 1841.

For Arms ſee page 33.

Hill, Colonel Richard Frederick, of Prees Hall, J.P. and D.L. for Co. Salop, Lieut.-Col. in the Army, Colonel of the Salop Militia (3rd son of the late John Hill, of Hawkeston), m. 1835 Maria Jane, only daug. of Major J. D. Bringhurst, and has issue—

William Frederick, b. 1843—Henry Philip, b. 1845.

Fanny Melita (who m. 1856 T. K. Gardner, Esq., of Leighton)—Mary Rhoda (who m. 1860 T. Meyrick, Esq., of Bush, Pembroke)—Selina Rachel (who m. 1864 the Rev. W. Wingfield, Vicar of Leighton)—Annette Catherine.

For Arms see Hill, of Hill Court, page 33.

Hill, Colonel George Staveley, of Peplow Hall, J.P. and D.L. for Co. Salop, Lieut.-Col. in the Army, and Lieut.-Col. in N. Salop Yeomanry (son of the late Colonel Sir Robert Chambre Hill, C.B., brother of Rowland, 1st Viscount Hill), m. 1832 Jane, daug. of Thomas Borough, Esq.

For Arms see Hill, of Hill Court, page 33.

Hill, Arthur Charles, formerly in the 16th Lancers, J.P. and D.L. for Co. Salop, and J.P. for Co. Worcester (son of the late Humphry Lowe, of Bromsgrove, by Lucy, d. and h. of the late Thomas Hill, of Court of Hill—assumed by Royal License his maternal name of Hill in 1865), m. 1st, 1841, Mary, daug. of Benjamin Flounders, Esq., of Culmington—who died 1844; 2nd, 1846, Caroline, daug. of Thomas

Baker, Efq., of Afhurft Lodge, Co. Kent—who died 1861, leaving iffue—

Arthur Hill, b. 1847 ;

3rd, 1867, Emma, widow of the late Thomas Longworth.

For Arms fee page 33.

How, Rev. William Walfham, Rector of Whittington (fon of the late William Wybergh How, of Shrewfbury, and defcended from John How (temp. Car. II.), m. 1849 Frances Anne, daug. of the Rev. Henry Douglas, Canon of Durham, and has iffue—

Frederick Douglas, b. 1853—Henry Walfham, b. 1856—Archibald Wybergh, b. 1858—Charles Chriftian, b. 1864.

Ellen Frances.

Arms: Arg., on a fefs fa., guttée d'or, three wolves' heads erafed of the fecond. Creft: A wolf's head erafed pean.

Hunt, Rowland, Efq., of Boreatton (fon of Rowland Hunt, and defcended from Richard de Venator, temp. Edw. I.), m. 1857 Florence Marianne, daug. of R. Humfrey, Efq., of Stoke Albany, and has iffue—

Rowland, b. 1858—Edward Rowland, b. 1859.

Arms: Per pale arg. and fa., a faltire counterchanged.
fejant fa., collared or., lined az., the line tied to a halb
fecond, headed of the laft.

Kenyon, Rev. Charles Orlando, Vicar of Great Neſs, R.D. (ſon of the Hon. Thomas Kenyon, of Pradoe, and deſcended from Lloyd, Lord Kenyon, Chief Juſtice of England), m. Matilda Eliſe, daug. of the Rev. Henry Calveley Cotton, of Great Neſs, and has iſſue—

Charles Robert Kenyon, b. 1845—Henry Thomas Kenyon, b. 1852.

Alice Matilda.

Arms: Sa., a chev. engr. or., betw. three croſſes flory arg. Creſt: A lion ſejant ppr., reſting the dexter paw on a croſs flory arg.

Kenyon-Slaney, William, Eſq., of Hatton Grange, J.P. and D.L. for Cos. Salop and Merioneth, Captain in the Indian Army retired, Captain N. Salop Yeomanry, late Lieut.-Colonel Shropſhire Rifle Volunteers (ſon of the Hon. Thomas Kenyon, of Pradoe, and deſcended from Lloyd, Lord Kenyon, Chief Juſtice of England), m. 1845 Frances Catherine, d. and co-h. of the late Robert Aglionby Slaney, M.P. for Shrewſbury, and has ſurviving iſſue—

William Slaney, b. 1847—Harry Conrad, b. 1850—Walter Rupert, b. 1851—Francis Gerald, b. 1858—Percy Robert, b. 1861.

Frances Edith—Agnes Charlotte—Katherine Maude—Violet Mabel.

Arms: Quarterly, 1ſt and 4th gu., a bend betw. three martlets erminois, for … a canton arg., for Slaney; 2nd and 3rd ſa., a chev. engr. … croſſes flory arg., for Kenyon. Creſts: Slaney— … gu., winged erminois, and gorged with a collar gemel … breaſt, for diſtinction, with a croſs croſslet of gold; … nt ppr., reſting the dexter paw on a croſs flory arg. … ms of Slaney.

Kittermaster, Rev. Frederick Wilfon, M.A., late Vicar of Edgton, Hon. Chaplain of the Shropfhire Artillery Volunteers, and Vicar of All Saints, Coventry (fon of James Kittermafter, M.D., of Meriden, Co. Warw., and defcended from William Kittermafter, of Romfley in Halefowen, and of Colefhill, Co. Warw., temp. Hen. VIII.), m. 1868 Rhoda Jane, daug. of the Rev. James Colley, Vicar of St. Julian's, Shrewfbury, and has iffue—

Frederick James, b. 1869.

Arms: Az., a chev. erminois betw. three bezants. Creft: On a chapeau az., turned up erm., an eagle with wings expanded erminois. Granted by Sir William Segar, Garter.

Leeke, Ralph Merrick, Efq., of Longford Hall, J.P. for Cos. Salop and Stafford, D.L. for Co. Salop, Sheriff 1850 (fon of Thomas Leeke, Efq., of Longford, and defcended from Ralph Leeke, of Ludlow, Ao. 1334), m. 1847 Lady Hefter Urania, daug. of Newton, 2nd Earl of Portfmouth, and has iffue—

Ralph, b. 1849—Thomas, b. 1854—Henry, b. 1856—William, b. 1862.

Hefter Catherine—Emily Dorothy—Charlotte Urania—Eveline Frances —Caroline Louifa.

Arms: Arg., on a chief gu., a fleur-de-lis or., over all a bend engr. az. Creft: A leg couped at the thigh charged with two fleurs-de-lis.

Legge, Hon. Arthur Charles, of Caynton, J.P. for Co. Salop, D.L. for Kent, Major-General in the Army (5th fon of George, 3rd Earl of Dartmouth) m. 1ft, 1827, Lady Anne Frederica, daug. of John, 1ft Earl _of Sheffield, who died 1829; 2nd, 1837, Caroline, daug. of the late James Charles Philip Bouwens, and has iſſue—

Charles, b. 1829—Rev. Alfred Arthur Kaye, b. 1839.

Alice Mary.

Arms: Az., a buck's head caboſſed arg. Creſt: Out of a ducal coronet or., a plume of five oſtrich feathers, three arg., two az.

𝕷𝖊𝖎𝖌𝖍𝖙𝖔𝖓, Sir Baldwin, of Loton Park, 7th Bart., Chairman of Quarter Seſſions and D.L. for Co. Salop (ſon of the late General Sir Baldwin Leighton, and deſcended from Tihel de Leton), ſuc. 1828, m. 1832 Mary, daug. of Thomas Netherton Parker, Eſq., of Sweeny, ſhe died 1864; and has iſſue—

Baldwin, b. 1836 (who m. 1864 Hon. Eleanor Leiceſter Warren, daug. of 2nd Baron de Tabley)—Stanley, b. 1837.

Frances Chriſtina (who m. Rev. Edward George Childe, Vicar of Kinlet and Rector of Cleobury Mortimer)—Iſabella (who m. 1ſt, 1858, Beriah Botfield, Eſq., M.P. for Ludlow, who died 1863; 2nd, 1866, A. Seymour, Eſq., M.P. for Totnes)—Charlotte—Margaret.

For Arms ſee page 42.

𝕷𝖑𝖔𝖞𝖉, Charles Spencer, Eſq., of Leaton Knolls, J.P. and D.L. for Co. Salop, Sheriff 1868 (ſon of Francis Lloyd, Eſq., of Domgay, Co. Montgomery, and of Leaton), ſuc. his brother 1864.

Heir Pres.: His nephew, Arthur Philip LLoyd, Eſq. (who m. 1863 Leila, daug. of Admiral the Hon. Charles Orlando Bridgeman, of Knockin, and has iſſue Arthur, b. 1864).

Arms: Per bend finiſter erm. and ermines, a lion ramp. or., and a border gu. Creſt: A demi-lion ramp. or.

Lovett, Major Thomas Heaton, of Belmont, J.P. for Co. Salop, Lieut-Col. Salop Rifle Volunteers, Major in the 98th Foot, retired (fon of the late Jofeph Venables Lovett, of Belmont), fuc. 1866, m. Cecil Elizabeth, daug. of Wilfon Jones, Efq., M.P., of Hartfheath Park, Co. Flint, and has iffue—

Hubert Richard, b. 1854—Henry Wilfon, b. 1853—Arthur, b. 1863.

Margaret Jofephine—Cecil Helen—Evelyn Grace—Mabel Beffie—Ethel Elizabeth.

Arms: Arg., three wolves paff. in pale fa. Creft: A wolf paff. ppr.

Mainwaring, Salufbury Kynafton, Efq., of Oteley Park, and of Bromborough Hall, Co. Chefter, J.P. for Co. Salop, and an Officer of the N. Salop Yeomanry (fon of the late Charles Kynafton Mainwaring, of Oteley), fuc. 1862, m. 1869 Edith Sarah, 2nd daug. of Sir Hugh Williams, Bart., of Bodelwyddan, Co. Flint.

Arms: Arg., two bars gu., quartering arg., a lion ramp, fa. Creft: Out of a ducal coronet or., an afs' head ppr.

More, Rev. Thomas Frederick, M.A., of Linley Hall (fon of the late Robert More, of Linley, Sheriff 1785, and defcended from Richard de la More, who came from Normandy with Duke William, and loft his life at the Battle of Haftings), m. 1831 his coufin Harriet Mary, daug. of Thomas More, Efq., and has iffue—

Robert Jafper, late M.P. for South Salop.

Harriet Louifa (who m. the Rev. Maurice Lloyd, Rector of Montgomery).

For Arms fee Moore, of Larden, page 48.

More, Rev. Robert Henry Gayer, M.A., of Larden Hall (fon of the late Thomas More, of Larden Hall, and defcended from William More, of Larden, 1491), fuc. 1804.

For Arms fee page 48.

Niccolls, William Henry, Efq., of Newnham (fon of the late William Owen Niccolls, of Shrewfbury and Hanwood, and defcended from Thomas Niccolls, Sheriff 1641, a fon of John Niccolls, of Boycott, Alderman of Shrewfbury, and Bailiff of the Town 1608), m. 1856 Lucy Strangward, daug. of the late Thomas Rogers, of Ofweftry, and has iffue—

John Henry, b. 1857—Dennys Rogers, b. 1858—William Owen Strangward, b. 1859—Walter, b. 1862—Alfred Edward, b. 1863—Roland, b. 1864.

Lucy Ellen.

For Arms fee page 50.

Owen, fee **Bulkeley-Owen**.

Pardoe, George, Efq., of Nafh Court, J.P. and D.L. for Co. Salop, and J.P. for Co. Worcefter (fon of the Rev. George Danfey Pardoe, of Nafh Court, and defcended from George Pardoe, of Cleeton, Ao. 1574), m. 1ft, 1843, Laura, daug. of the late Thomas White, of Bognor; 2nd, Mary Elizabeth, only daug. of the late Fielden Croome, of Cirencefter.

Heir Pres.: His brother Henry, b. 1817.

Arms: Arg., on a crofs counter-componée or. and gu., in the firft quarter a water bouget, in the fecond an eagle difplayed, in the third a fwan, in the fourth an efcallop, all fa., on a chief az., a lion pafs. guard. of the firft. Creft: A demi-lion ramp. guard. arg., holding an efcallop fa.

Percy, Algernon Charles Heber, Efq., of Hodnet Hall, and of Armine, Yorkfhire, J.P. and D.L. for Co. Salop, Captain of Rifle Volunteers (fon of the late Hon. and Right Rev. Hugh Percy, Bifhop of Carlifle, and defcended from the Percys, Earls of Northumberland, whofe anceftor, William de Percy, accompanied William the Conqueror), m. 1839 Emily, daug. of the Right Rev. Reginald Heber, Bifhop of Calcutta, and niece of Richard Heber, of Hodnet, whofe eftate fhe inherited, and has iffue—

Algernon, b. 1845 (and who m. 1867 his coufin, Alice Charlotte Mary, only child of the late Rev. F. V. Lockwood)—Reginald Joceline, b. 1849—Hugh Louis, b. 1852—Henry Vernon, b. 1858—Alan William, b. 1865.

Blanche Emily—Ellen Cecilia—Agnes Katherine—Maude Ellen—Gertrude Amelia—Evelyn Mary—Ifabel Harriet.

Arms: Thofe of Percy, of Northumberland; on an efcutcheon of pretence the arms of Heber.

Perry, Mrs., of Bryn Tanat, Co. Montgomery (eldeft daug. of the late Rev. John Eyton, Rector of Wellington, and grand-daughter of Thomas Eyton, of Eyton, Sheriff 1779, who was defcended from Robert de Eyton, of Eyton, temp. Hen. II.), m. 1835 William Henry Perry, Efq., of Shrewfbury, and by him, who died 1854, had iffue three fons and four daughters, of whom furvive—

Mary Betfy (who m. 1857 Henry Leflie, Efq., and has iffue three fons and one daughter)—Rofe Maria.

Arms: Perry impaling Eyton—for the latter fee page 25.

𝔓𝔩𝔬𝔴𝔡𝔢𝔫, William Henry Francis, Efq., of Plowden Hall, Sheriff 1848 (fon of the late William Plowden, of Plowden, and defcended from Roger de Plowden, who ferved under King Richard in the Crufades), fuc. 1838 his uncle Edmund, m. Barbara, daug. of Francis Cholmeley, of Brandfby Hall, Co. York, and has furviving iffue—

William Francis, b. 1853.
Barbara Mary—Ellinor—Conftance—Gertrude Mary—Sibyl Maria—Laura Mary.
For Arms fee page 55.

𝔓𝔬𝔴𝔦𝔰.—Edward James Herbert, 3rd Earl of Powis, of Walcot, and of Powis Caftle, Co. Montgomery, J.P. and D.L. for Co. Salop, J.P. and D.L. and Chairman of Quarter Seffions for Co. Montgomery (fon of Edward Herbert, K.G., 2nd Earl, and grandfon of Edward, 2nd Lord Clive, who in 1784 m. Henrietta Antonia, f. and h. of George Edward Henry Arthur, laft Earl of Powis, of the family of Herbert, and was in 1804 elevated to the Earldom of Powis). The before-named Edward, 2nd Lord Clive, was defcended from the Clives, of Styche, fettled there in the reign of Hen. II. The prefent Earl of Powis fucceeded in 1848.

Heir Pres.: His brother, the Right Hon. Sir Percy Egerton, K.C.B., M.P. for South Salop.
Arms: Per pale az. and gu., three lions ramp. arg.
For Arms of Clive, fee page 17.
Creations: Lord Clive, of Plaffey, in the Peerage of Ireland, 1762; Lord Clive, in the Peerage of England, 1794; Earl of Powis, Vifcount Clive, 1804.

Purton, Thomas Pardoe, Efq., of Faintree Hall, J.P. for Co. Salop (fon of the late William Purton), m. 1831 Caroline Frances, daug. of Lionel Lampet, Efq., and has iffue—

William Cecil Pardoe, b. 1835 (who m. 1862 Frances Elizabeth, only daug. of John Browne Twift, Efq., of Stoke Houfe, Co. Warw.)

Caroline Hefter (who m. the Rev. John Smyth Purton, Rector of Chetton.

Arms: Arg., on a chev. gu., three pears or. Creft: On a mount vert, a pear tree fructed ppr.

Rocke, John, Efq., of Clungunford Houfe, J.P. and D.L. for Co. Salop, Lieut. S. Salop Yeomanry, Sheriff 1869 (fon of the Rev. John Rocke, of Clungunford, defcended from John Rocke, of Shrewfbury, Ao. 1230, and Pr. Rep. of the family), fuc. 1849, m. 1853 Conftance Anne, daug. of Sir Charles Cuyler, Bart., of St. John's Lodge, Co. Herts, and has furviving iffue—

John Charles Levifon, b. 1855.

Conftance Ida.

For Arms fee page 58.

Salwey, John, Efq., of Moor Park (fon of Richard Salwey, Efq., of Moor Park, and defcended from Geoffrey de Saleway, of Norton-under-Cannoc, Co. Stafford, temp. Hen. III.), m. 1843, Harriet Anne, daug. of Thomas Bourke Ricketts, of Combe Houfe, Co. Hereford.

Arms: Sa., a faltire engr. or. Creft: A demi-Moor wreathed about the temples arg. and fa., a belt from the finifter fhoulder to the dexter hip az.

𝕾𝖆𝖓𝖉𝖋𝖔𝖗𝖉, Thomas Hugh, Efq., of Sandford, J.P. and D.L. for Co. Salop, J.P. for Chefhire, Captain N. Salop Yeomanry, Sheriff 1866 (fon of the late Thomas Hugh Sandford, of Sandford, defcended from Richard de Sandford, Lord of Sandford 1167, and Pr. Rep. of the family), fuc. 1825, m. 1ft, 1849, Alexina, daug. of the Hon. Charles Lindfay (fhe died 1851); 2nd, Sarah Halfted, daug. of William Halfted Poole, Efq., of Terrick.

For Arms fee page 59.

𝕾𝖆𝖓𝖉𝖋𝖔𝖗𝖉, Humphrey, Efq., of the Ifle, Barrifter-at-Law, J.P. for Co. Salop (fon of the late Rev. Humphrey Sandford, of the Ifle, and defcended from Nicholas Sandford, of Calverhall, 3rd fon of Nicholas Sandford, Lord of Sandford, temp. Hen. VI.), m. 1852 Anne Taylor, 5th daug. of Jofeph Armitage, Efq., of Milnfbridge Houfe, Co. York, and has iffue—

Humphrey, b. 1856—Folliott, b. 1859—Richard, b. 1863.

Frances Holland—Annette Armine—Ada Roffall—Margaret Plowden.

For Arms fee page 59.

𝕾𝖈𝖔𝖙𝖙, George Jonathan, Efq., of Betton le Strange, J.P. for Co. Merioneth, Sheriff for fame Co. 1844) fon of the late George Scott, of Betton le Strange, and defcended from Richard Scott, temp. Eliz.), m. 1840 Augufta Frances, daug. of William Wynne, Efq., of Peniarth, Co. Merioneth, and has furviving iffue—

Louifa Sydney (who m. 1868 Major William Eddington Stuart, 15th Huffars).

Arms: Arg., three Catherine wheels fa., two and one, within a border engr. gu. Creft: A demi-griffin fegreant fa., membered gu.

Selwyn, Rev. William, Vicar of Bromfield (fon of the Right Rev. George Auguftus Selwyn, D.D., Lord Bifhop of Lichfield, and late Bifhop of New Zealand), m. 1864 Harriet Sufan, daug. of the Rev. Ambrofe Steward, of Leekford Hall, Suffolk, and has iffue—

William George, b. 1865.

Harriet Alice.

Severne, John Edmund, Efq., of Wallop Hall, J.P. and D.L. for Cos. Salop and Northampton, J.P. for Co. Montgomery, late Captain 16th Light Dragoons (fon of the late John Michael Severne, of Thenford, and defcended from John Severne, of Shrawley, temp. Hen. VIII.), m. 1858 Florence Morgan, daug. of the Very Rev. Hugh Uffher Tighe, Dean of Ardagh.

Heir Pres.: His brother Arthur, Rector of Thenford, b. 1827.

Arms: Arg., on a chev. fa., nine bezants or. Creft: A cinquefoil or.

Sitwell, William Willoughby George Hurt, Efq., of Ferney Hall, J.P. and D.L. for Co. Hereford, Lieut. S. Salop Yeomanry, Sheriff 1858 (fon of Francis Hunt Sitwell, of Ferney), m. 1858 Eliza Harriet, daug. of Richard Burton Phillipfon, Efq., of Dunfton Houfe, Co. Stafford, and has iffue—

Francis Hurt, b. 1860.

Ellinor Harriet Hurt.

Arms: Barry of eight or. and vert, three lions ramp. fa. Creft: A demi-lion ramp. erafed fa., holding betw. the paws an efcutcheon per pale or, and vert,

Smythe, Lieut.-Col. Thomas, of Hilton, late of the Royal Madras Engineers, now commanding 3rd Battalion of Staffordſhire Rifle Volunteers (ſon of the late John Groom Smythe, of Hilton, and deſcended from Thomas le Smythe, of Hutton or Hilton, temp. Edw. III.), m. 1857 Mary, only child of the late Admiral Deans, of Cheltenham, and has iſſue—

Mary Eliza Clio—Cecilia Ann Parke—Anne Blanche.

Arms: Sa., a bend betw. ſix martlets arg. Creſt: A buffalo's head ppr.

Stubbs, William, Eſq., of Beckbury Hall, J.P. for Co. Salop (ſon of the late Walter Stubbs, and deſcended from Walter Stubbs, of Beckbury, Ao. 1660, who m. a daug. of Sir J. Aſtley, of Pattſhul Park), m. 1838 Elizabeth, daug. of John Stanier, Eſq., of Leaton.

Heir: His nephew.

Arms: Sa., on a bend or., betw. three pheons arg., as many buckles gu. Creſt: A buck's head caboſſed.

Sutherland.—George Granville William Sutherland Leveſon Gower, 3rd Duke of Sutherland, Lord Lieutenant of Cos. Sutherland and Cromarty (ſon of George, 2nd Duke, and deſcended from Sir Allan Gower, Lord of Sittenham in Yorkſhire, at the time of the Conqueſt), ſuc. 1861, m. 1849 Ann, only child of John Hay-Mackenzie, Eſq., of Newhall and Cromartie (created Counteſs of Cromartie 1862), and has ſurviving iſſue—

Cromartie, Marquis of Stafford, b. 1851—Francis, Viſcount Tarrat, b. 1852.

Florence—Alexandra, for whom the Princeſs of Wales was ſponſor.

Creations: Baronet, 1620; Baron, 1703; Earl, 1746; Marquis, 1786; Duke 1833.

Arms of Gower: Barry of eight arg. and gu., over all a crofs patonce fa. Creft: A wolf pafs. arg., collared and lined or.

For Arms of Levefon fee page 43.

Thorneycroft, Thomas, Efq., of Hadley Park, and of Tettenhall, Co. Stafford, J.P. and D.L. for Co. Stafford, Sheriff of fame Co. 1864, J.P. for Co. Salop, Major of Stafford Yeomanry (fon of the late George Benjamin Thorneycroft, of Hadley Park), m. 1847 Jane, daug. of A. Whitelaw, Efq., and has iffue—

George Benjamin, b. 1849—James Baird, b. 1851—Hamo Douglas, b. 1855—Alexander Whitelaw, b. 1859—Wallace, b. 1864.

Jeffie—Jeannie—Eleanor—Florence.

Arms: Vert, a mafcle or., betw. four crofs crofflets arg. Creft: On a mural crown gu., a falcon volant ppr., jeffed membered and beaked or., betw. two palm branches of the laft.

Thursby-Pelham, Rev. Henry, M.A., of Cound Hall (fon of the Rev. George Auguftus Thurfby, took the additional name of Pelham 1852 in right of his mother, co-heirefs of John Creffett Pelham, Efq.), m. 1827 Mary Elizabeth, daug. of Thomas Papillon, Efq., of Acrife, Kent, and has furviving iffue—

Walter, b. 1830 (who m. 1865 Emily Fitzgerald, daug. of the Hon. James Butler, and has iffue Walter Henry, b. 1867)—Auguftus, Rector of Cound, b. 1832 (who m. 1863 Adelaide Eunice, daug. of the Rev. P. S. Wilkinfon, of Mount Ofwald, Durham)—Francis, b. 1838 (who m. 1866 Mary, widow of — Nicholls, Efq.)—Pelham, b. 1840, Captain in H.M. 30th Foot—Creffett, b. 1843 (who m. 1869 Conftance Emily, daug. of Hugh Davies-Griffith, Efq., of Caer-Rhyn, Carnarvonfhire).

Arms: Az., three pelicans arg., vulning themfelves ppr. Creft: A peacock in his pride ppr.

Vaughan, Robert Chambre, Efq., of Burlton Hall (fon of
Captain Thomas Vaughan, of Burlton, and defcended
from Philip Vaughan, who m. 1716 Jane, daug. of
Roger Bolas, and grand-daug. of Arthur Chambre, of
Burlton), m. 1828 Anna, daug. of the Hon. Edward
Maffey, and has iffue—

John Nanney Chambre, b. 1830—Edward Goldifborough Chambre,
b. 1832—Arthur Chicheley Chambre, b. 1834—William Wynn,
b. 1843.

Catherine Elizabeth—Anna—Edith—Lowry.

Arms: Arg., on a chev. betw. three boars' heads, couped gu., armed or.,
a crefcent of the field within an annulet of the laft. Creft: On a chapeau
a boar's head, couped gu., armed or., langued az.

For Arms of Chambre fee page 14.

Walcot, Rev. Charles, of Bitterley Court, J.P. for Co.
Salop (fon of the Rev. John Walcot, of Bitterley, and
defcended from John Walcot, of Walcot, temp.
Hen. V., a defcendant of David ap Rees, Lord of
Garthmael, who m. Jane, d. and h. of Sir John
Walcot), m. 1ft, 1818, Anne, daug. of Major William
Walcot, of Terry Park, Co. Dublin, who left iffue—

John, b. 1820 (who m. 1844 Mary Sophia, daug. of Sir Thomas Phillips,
of Middle Hall, Co. Worcefter)—Charles Thomas, b. 1821—William
Henry, b. 1823;

2nd, 1827, Charlotte, daug. of John Molyneux, of
Ludlow, who left iffue—

Reginald Herbert, b. 1855;

3rd, Mary Anne, daug. of the Rev. John Rocke, of
Clungunford Houfe.

For Arms fee page 67.

𝔚𝔞𝔩𝔣𝔬𝔯𝔡, John Henſhaw Nickſon, M.A., Ruyton Towers, Shrewſbury, Roden Houſe, Wem, and Treago, Roſs, J.P. for Co. Hereford, Cornet in the North Salopian Yeomanry (ſon of the late John Henſhaw Walford), m. 1862 Mary, only child of William Staley, Eſq., of Thiſtlemount, Roſſendale, Lancaſhire, and has iſſue—

John Aſhton Henſhaw, b. 1863—Thomas Walford Henſhaw, b. 1866.

Mary Joan Henſhaw.

𝔚𝔞𝔯𝔱𝔢𝔯, Henry De Grey, Eſq., of Longden Manor, D.L. and J.P. for Co. Salop (ſon of the late Henry De Grey Warter, of Cruck Meole, and deſcended from Richard Wartyr, Sheriff of York 1431, twice Lord Mayor thereof, viz., 1436 and 1451, and M.P. for that City 13 Hen. VI.), m. 1833 Harriet, daug. of John Bembow, Eſq., M.P. for Dudley, and has iſſue—

Henry De Grey, b. 1834.

Elizabeth Mary (who m. 1860 Meaburn, ſon of Meaburn Tatham, Eſq., of Highgate, Middleſex, and nephew of the late Ralph Tatham, D.D., Maſter of St. John's Coll., Cambidge, and has ſurrviving iſſue, Henry De Grey Warter, b. 1862, and four daughters).

Arms : Sa., on a chev. engr. betw. three cheſs rooks arg., as many croſſes croſllet fitchée of the firſt.

𝔚𝔞𝔰𝔢𝔶, Rev. William George Leigh, M.A., Vicar of Quatford and Morville cum Aſton Eyre (ſon of the Rev. George Waſey, B.D., of Wardington, and deſcended from Robert Waſey, of North Walſham,

temp. Car. II.), m. 1844 Eliza Leonora, daug. of the
late Philip Monkton, of the Bengal Civil Service,
and has iſſue—

Sophia Honoria—Leonora Sabrina.

Arms: Or., on a croſs ſa., five bezants betw. four ermine ſpots. Creſt:
A falcon riſing or., beaked membered and collared ſa., the collar charged
with three bezants, belled or.

Granted by John Anſtis, Garter, Aug. 12, 1729.

Wenlock.—Sir Beilby Richard Lawley, 2nd Lord Wenlock,
of Bourton Cottage, Wenlock, and Eſcrick Park, York,
and Canwell Hall, Tamworth, J.P. for North and
Eaſt Riding, and Lord Lieutenant for Eaſt Riding,
York (ſon of Beilby, 1ſt Lord, and deſcended from
Thomas Lawley, couſin and heir of John, Lord
Wenlock, Privy Councillor to King Edw. IV.),
ſuc. 1852, m. 1846 Lady Elizabeth, daug. of Richard,
2nd Marquis of Weſtminſter, and has iſſue—

Beilby, b. 1849—Richard Thompſon, b. 1856—Algernon George,
b. 1857—Arthur, b. 1860—Robert, b. 1863.

Caroline Elizabeth—Alethea Jane—Conſtance Mary—Katherine.

Creations: Baronet, 1641; Baron, 1839.

For Arms ſee page 41.

Whitmore, Rev. George, of Stockton, J.P. for Co. Salop
(2nd ſon of the late Thomas Whitmore, of Apley),
m. 1848 Sarah, daug. of the late John Deacon, of
Mabledon, Kent, and has ſurviving iſſue—

Algernon George Bernard, b. 1849—Henry Eardley, b. 1855.

Katharine Mildred—Dora Louiſa Mary—Geraldine Ellen Georgina.

For Arms ſee page 71.

Whitmore, Rev. Francis Henry Wolryche-, of Dudmaston, J.P. for Co. Salop (son of the late Rev. Francis Laing, of the Mythe, Co. Gloucester), assumed 1864 the name of Wolryche-Whitmore, m. 1845 Isabella, daug. of Captain Henry Bazely, R.N., and has issue—

Francis Alexander, b. 1845—Malcolm, b. 1849—Henry Bazely, b. 1856. Isabel Louisa.

For Arms see page 71.

Winder, Uvedale Corbett, Esq., of Cotsbrook, J.P. and D.L. for Co. Salop, Recorder of Bridgnorth and Wenlock (son of the late Ven. Archdeacon Corbett, of Longnor, and descended through the female line from Sir Edward Corbett, Bart., of Longnor, Ao. 1642, assumed in 1869 the name of Winder), m. 1817 Mary Anne, only daug. of Joseph Lyon, Esq., of Ashfield, Co. Chester, and has surviving issue—

Uvedale, b. 1818 (who m. 1848 Mary, daug. of John Fryer, Esq., of the Wergs, Co. Stafford, and has issue four sons)—William, b. 1820 (a Major in the Army, and of Vaenor Park, Co. Montgomery)—Robert, b. 1821 (in Holy Orders, who m. 1844 Maria, daug. of John Pountney, Esq., of Lowe Hill, Co. Stafford, and has issue two sons and a daughter)—John, b. 1822 (who m. 1864 Georgina Grace, daug. of George Holmes, Esq., of Brook Hall, Co. Norfolk, and has issue two sons and two daughters)—Lionel, b. 1831 (Rector of Pontesbury, who m. 1861 Frances Harriet, daug. of the Rev. Robert Hornby, of Lythwood Hall, she died 1865, leaving issue two daughters).

Mary Elizabeth (who m. 1847 Daniel Bennett, Esq., of Farringdon House, Co. Berks, and has issue one daughter, Mildred Ann).

Arms: Winder quartering Corbett, of Longnor; for the latter see page 18.

𝖂𝖎𝖓𝖌𝖋𝖎𝖊𝖑𝖉, Charles George, Efq., of Onflow Hall, J.P. for Co. Salop (fon of the late Rev. Charles Wingfield, of the Gro, Co. Montgomery), fuc. his uncle 1862, m. 1865 Jane Mary Anne, daug. of Clopton Wingfield, Efq., of the Rhyfnant.

Arms: Arg., on a bend finifter gu., cotifed fa., three pairs of wings conjoined of the field. Creft: A high bonnet or cap per pale fa. and arg., banded gu., betw. two wings difplayed, all guttée counterchanged.

𝖂𝖔𝖔𝖉, Rev. Robert Faulkner, Rector of Moreton Corbet (fon of the late Thomas Wood, of Harcourt Oak), m. 1861 Mariamne Sophia, daug. of John Edward Mofley, Efq., of Sans Souci, and has iffue—

Zoe Florence—Grace Caroline.

Arms: Three demi-woodmen pp. Creft: A pelican ppr.

W. R. KING, PRINTER, SWAN PASSAGE, BIRMINGHAM.